Island Journeys

Island Journeys

A Countrywoman's Travels by
BESSIE SKEA

**THE
ORKNEY
PRESS**

For my great-grandchildren;
in memory of an almost-recent Orkney
that was good in its time

Published in 1993 by The Orkney Press Ltd
12 Craigiefield Park, St Ola, Kirkwall, Orkney

ISBN 0 907618 29 4

Book design by Iain Ashman

Typesetting by Karen Munn

Set in 12/13 Bookman

Printed by The Orcadian Ltd
The Kirkwall Press, Victoria Street, Kirkwall, Orkney

Published with the financial support of
The Scottish Arts Council and
Orkney Islands Council.

Contents

Foreword

*B*essie Skea (Bessie Grieve) will always be remembered as one of Orkney's foremost nature writers.

Orkney has always had plenty of naturalists, from Rev. George Low of Birsay and Rev. George Barry of Shapinsay nearly two hundred years ago. The contribution of such men, and those who followed them, right up to the present day, is invaluable.

What Bessie Skea has contributed to the web is a thread of lyricism. She knows the flowers and birds and shells of Orkney as well as anybody, but she looks at them through the eye of a poet.

From her house at the very centre of Orkney, Hillview in Harray, Bessie over the decades has made frequent forays among the islands, and she has written about them well, chiefly in a weekly column in *The Orcadian* (many people's favourite read in that paper). Those journeys have never been just an outing for Bessie; everywhere she has brought a sympathetic and lyrical eye to bear. It is all so much more memorable than aiming a camera here and there, for the essence of the place has been evoked (a thing that casual photography can rarely do).

Readers worldwide will share Bessie Skea's vivid enjoyment of nature and the spirit of place in this book from The Orkney Press.

The text is enhanced by Isobel Gardner's excellent drawings.

George Mackay Brown
Stromness
29 October 1992

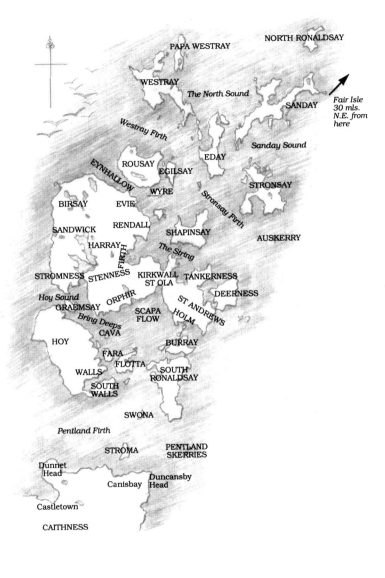

Ice on the Loch of Wasdale

A week ago, on a mild grey day when the land lay heavy and sticky with melt-water, I walked towards the loch. Hoy was still streaked with snow, hard-driven into sheer gullies on the face of the Ward Hill; banks of soft cloud built themselves out of hilltop air and trailed along the ranges of Hoy and Orphir, moving, as did the chimney-reek, on a breeze from the east. Clover-leaves and moss on the road-verge were dew-silvered. In our quarry-pool, ice, shrunken and submerged, hid the coppery leaves of water-weeds. Drift-ice had collected along the far side of the Stenness Loch, and dykes held hard-packed, white snow along their northern borders. A quality of the air suggested that winter was only in abeyance and that the ice-lowsing was not yet complete.

Our black cat hunted the road-verge ahead.

1

The gate of the field leading towards the Loch of Wasdale was shut, hitched to a corner-post wearing lichen-leaves of grey. Soft ice lay in the ditch, but the mud underfoot was infinitely colder than the previous snow, and clung chillingly to my boots. A corbie rose and winged away. Field and park were sheep-hoof-dented; black tracks converged by the connecting gate where only spurting mud remained.

Moss, bright-green-fronded, and in soft green cushions, grew with lichens on the north face of the dyke. This is their season. Dull-green lichens pushed through thin grass, and the second corner-post wore tufts of grey-green and lime-green, with several spots of bright orange. Those on the stones spread in patches of yellow, flakes and beards of grey, some with little stalked cups, in perpendicular fairy forests.

Heather was bushy and dark green, and on the deep ditch-side was a stark forest of meadow-sweet with dockans and hogweed.

The loch lay white-calm with grey ice-floes at its centre. There stood a multitude of water-fowl, looking very large. The crow had warned them of my approach; flock by flock they lifted, calling, to settle farther away beyond the islet. An outstretched heron lay dead by the shore.

Leaves of celandine shone spring-green, and ragwort, which never gives up, grew beside the over-wintering leaves of primrose on the bank.

Vole tracks cut through the short turf right to the water's edge, and rabbits had left brown excavations in the grassy face. Willows, their feet in the water, wore buds on pliant green and brown stems; and some of these retained last season's leaves, still soft and firmly attached, in umber and grey-brown shades. Ice sheets lay tossed ashore. The skeleton of a beaked creature pointed towards the water. Overhead sounded a rush of wings, the drone of an aircraft mingling with the apprehensive departure of another contingent of ducks. Many cartridge cases lay along the shore; the birds had learned wariness and even feared the approach of a prowler with a pencil.

A trout leapt with a silver splash. A wind sighed down from the hill as I left the loch and stepped over a fence into a cold bog, dark with dried meadowsweet, sharp with grey thistles, and rustling with reeds.

On the slope of a stubble-field were silver-haired seedling thistles, like landfast starfish, and the earth made small sucking, gurgling noises, as though a thousand throats drank moisture. This thaw-sodden land was more inhospitable than fields of snow had been; it struck through my boots and urged me on. A snow-bunting flashed white wings across the dyke.

Leaning on mossy stones, I looked back across the valley. Our light-green, shiny roof blended quite well into its surroundings when viewed from this vantage-point. Cars moved sleekly along the roads. Above, on the face of the hill, was a knowe within a hollow, a smoothly-rounded hillock, surrounded by heather and whins. Dry red-brown ferns were crumpled along the dyke, but green-gold fronds remained fresh nearby, and claytonia leaves shone darkly green under smooth-barked trees with black buds. A black cat vanished over the dyke.

A nest, constructed from heather-twigs, perched in a leafless tree. A few uneaten rose-hips clung drily to bushes. Rhododendron leaves of polished green, and a dark-green monkey-

3

puzzle tree, brightened the wintry plantation. A strange fungoid growth, in stacked layers of green, grew from a tree-stump. Lichens bearded the bark of living trees, and another toadstool-fungus projected like shelves from its host.

By the plantation path bushes held bright orange-gold leaves, and a lovely conifer, in the new part of the wood, grew tall and full-needled in lush green, and bore small cones. On the ground lay several red berries, well away from the only holly bushes within sight. Rabbits flashed white tails up the hill, and birds disappeared as I drew near. I had alarmed every furred and feathered creature in the area, and felt very much an intruder. The path was dank and slippery underfoot. Over the dyke, I could see the flooded, ice-sheeted valley, through which ran a white-foaming, loudly-rushing burn.

In a carpet of fallen foliage rose the small green heart-leaves of celandine, to gild the entire forest floor in the spring before the leaves again appear on the trees. Golden saxifrage spread by the path, but I looked in vain for any flowering plant until, near the east gate, there appeared a single daisy lifting from the mud with its eye closed.

By the brig, as I watched the water, a bonny bird exploded from my feet; a woodcock, patterned in brown and russet, short-tailed and thick-bodied, it vanished among the rising trees.

Having seen my first wild flower of the year, I turned towards home. A wren flew scolding past, and wood pigeons called.

Several heather-built nests were revealed on bare branches, and one was now completely covered with living moss, of soft, velvety green. I stood between the dykes, watching the burn go by, while bird-voices and wings passed above the trees. Another plane, on some high errand, trailed its sound across the sky.

A Windward Shore

Out of all the fine Sundays that have punctuated the mild winter, our early Field Club outings happened to be grey. The February trip was cancelled, in one of the bitterest easterly gales of the year, and although the March excursion was less unfavourable it was not a day for undue lingering along a windward shore. A bitter air-stream came clouding in from the south-east, bringing foot-cold and eye-streaming weather.

We were late in setting out, owing to one of these incidents infrequent in this mechanically-minded household - the car ignition had been left switched on overnight. Calling all hands we got the vehicle started by pushing it down the road.

By the Brig o' Waithe we found that the Field Club had arrived in force, and in many colours

7

to brighten the drab day. The tide was out; a fire hazed the sea, reeking from the Orphir shore. Behind us, down the channel and around the point, came a gay red-sailed boat, lifting on the waves. It was a brisk day for sailing among the whitecaps, and the air was fresh to walk in. All through the redware and under the stones lived a small multitude, creeping in algae undergrowth, wriggling, sidling, and siphoning their way along. We raised the roofs of their worlds which caused some consternation among the more mobile. There ensued a swift closing of anemone tentacles, a 'playing possum' of captured crabs and sea slaters, a wild squirming of swirdos. But it was not a day designed for lengthy contemplation. The rock slabs were carefully replaced and we moved on.

Random fossils strewed the shore, dark blue bony plates fused forever into stone. Great is the fascination in rocks, because underfoot lies our entire world history if we could but read it accurately. Here is a 'dyke' pushed up from molten depths when the unstable rock-crust slipped; here is a piece of lava, porous as sea-foam; here are sun-cracks forming pleasing patterns in two colours, telling of the earth that heaved to lift the lake-bottom mud to face the searing sun and, later, let it sink again, to leave a new deposit laid with careless artistry in the seams.

There are other patterns, appearng as tree-roots or branches because they are darker and have a core - these have pushed up from below when the surface cracked. Ripples have marked these cool blue flags when they were soft shore-sand, when the sea that came and went was even less predictable than it is now, when continents were in the making and moved on shifting plasma in the depths. Here is a petrified pebble-bed; there is a fault with vertical strata. All these can be found on any shore.

By the time we had reached the Bu of Cairston I was heavily laden, having collected every bonny stone I could carry. They rattled in my shoulder-bag against my glasses-case and books; they weighed down both pockets of my coat; granite jostled marl and conglomerates.

Now, on the edge of the banks undercut by the sea, were the foundations of a broch; the remains of a Viking castle dyked the yard at the other side of the farm, yellow and green with close lichen, tufted and branched with grey. Hens scratched where earls have feasted. The farm buildings have grown from the stones of broch and castle.

Over the centuries many nations' ships have come and gone, sheltering by these shores their tall masts or square sails; and in pre-Viking days, doubtless the howe-dwellers patrolled this haven, for they were sea-farers too.

On the shore lay a storm-tossed guillemot, soft of plumage and limp, buffeted by the wild seas that had beaten against our eastern seaboard for weeks, casting fresh fish and clean wood up on land. Other flotsam, borne from who knows where, was threaded among the stones; eelgrass, some with roots attached, some only shiny green ribbon-foliage. Sea-squirts, strange red purse-like creatures, were gathered up by delighted bairns.

From the red-ware rocks a head came up to watch us, and a decrepit-looking skarf fluttered towards the sea. A discussion followed as to whether such rock-bound skarfs came ashore to die or to moult. This one ran slowly away and

9

did not attempt to return to the water even when pounced upon and captured; it was a shag, with metallic green plumage and denuded of its natural oils. It sat down calmly when released.

As we retuned to the car I picked up more stone slabs, inlaid ochre on blue, as if random, twigs and petals had been trapped. These did not have the appearance of suncracks, neither were they fossils.

In a grey, inclement evening we went home.

Roads and
Shores of the West

Grey clouds are moving fast, and the easterly wind is sighing in under doors and sifting through every chink and cranny. The nights have been frosty of late, and last evening I saw the new moon in a clear sky. The weekend gave us several fine and spring-like days, and on the 1st of April we went out to look at the western sea. Our roses and flowering currant were in green bud, and a few low polyanthus were in flower. Daffodils remained in the bud stage, with just the folded petal-tips showing through. The earth was drying rapidly. The moorland lay in dingy tones of withered grass and brown heather, with gulls and oystercatchers in residence. The sun turned the greener fields to gold, but the grass was slow in rising. Yellow crocuses lifted silken cups to the sun near the Stoneyhill Road, and at Tormiston the daffodils and

11

narcissi were getting ready to open.

Several fishermen wearing waders were emerging from a car on the Brodgar Road. Swans, and fully-grown cygnets, sailed offshore, and oystercatchers waded among the stones and rushes in the water's edge. Two dead swans lay near the Sentinel Stone.

The Stenness loch shone in the sun; Harray's rippled water was blue. Coltsfoot and an occasional dandelion gave gleams of gold; farther on, we saw a row of daffodils in flower in the edge of a ploughed field, where the land lies to the sun and catches a double dose of sunshine where the loch throws back the light. A patch of colour near the old mill proved to be nets strung on poles to dry. Rabbits sat in the fields along the road to Yesnaby, alert, with ears high. In the reedy swamp many birds were nesting and fending, with black-headed gulls and curlews predominant. Linnets, with red fronts, flew from a fence. The sea shone, outlining the Brough and the cliffs ahead in silver.

There were few cars in the parking-space and walkers here and there on the clifftop in the distance. At one time we could take a car downhill, past the primula scotica area, to within easy reach of the fishing rock that looks out on to the Brough; but now there is a pin afore the neb of any car wanting access: thus a pleasant sheltered geo and an interesting shore is restricted to the able-bodied only. That car-track had been in use for many years, and it was well back from the piece of craig subject to rockfalls. I have walked down the track several times since the barrier went there, but my man says, sadly, that he will never be able to get down there again.

The Scottish hills were mist-pale on the

skyline, and Hoy rose lavender-blue, with a dusting of snow on the height of the Kame. The air must have been colder to the west, because the snow had gone from the Ward Hill and the Cuilags. The sea was flat and blue to the horizon, with an occasional dark flurry where a vagrant wind ran over it, and a single oily trail like that left by a shoal of mackerel, running off-shore.

Whaups watched our progress, and oyster-catchers prodded the earth as we drove on towards Skaill. A stubble field had been ploughed and was drying rapidly, and here we were assailed by a pungent smell of dung. This odour promised fertility, but it got into the car with us, and remained there for miles. The Loch of Skaill lipped the road-edge; primroses and daffodils opened on the banks, and goldeneye ducks swam on the loch. Kye and calves occupied a sandy field. We found a neat parking space at the Bay of Skaill, artistically delineated by a foot-high palisade of slant-topped posts. But we went on to a favourite stopping-place on the old road below the kirkyard, where we looked out on the low tide rocks that ran in ridges far out into the bay, and on a light square on the headland that was the Hole o' Rowe with reflected sun-shine coming through. People walked on the sands; bairns and dogs ran races. Our last visit to this shore had been in the past summer, when rock pools and ridges were tenanted by dunter ducks with ducklings, who dabbled happily. No ducks were to be seen on Sunday; I assume they were ashore, nesting. And that, of course, explains the apparent mystery of the large proportion of oiled drakes reported recently. The only time of year when ducks and drakes congregate in equal numbers is in the

13

mating season; as soon as nesting begins they separate, and the drakes flock out to sea again. Eiders with young later frequent the shores. Rafts of drakes may be seen at sea, and that is where these unfortunates have become contaminated with oil. Their wives would have been safely ashore at the time.

When I was peedie, there were always eider ducks in the bay; but I never even saw a drake until after I left Shapinsay, and then I was amazed at its beauty, wondering how the male and female of the species could be so different in appearance. In the 'fifties I not only began to notice them in the String - where no doubt they had been all along although I had not previously had the eyes to see them - but I spotted a king eider, which I was hesitant about claiming as a positive sighting because these were not supposed to be seen so far south....

In Sandwick and Birsay we saw daffodils, and coltsfoot in constellations. Primroses peeped through grass here and there. The lagoon of Choin in Marwick had ebbed, but two swans sailed there, and a pair of shelduck, most beautiful of all the ducks, swam out from the shore at the sight of us. The grass was green on Marwick, and there were daisies opening to the light. Good black land had been deeply ploughed. From the brae of Harpsa we saw a ship beyond the Brough coming south, her superstructure blindingly white. Rocks, dark with weed, were bare far out in the bay. Black cattle grazed on the links, and along the sandy shore.

A rowing boat moved swiftly on Boardhouse Loch. The plantation on Ravie Hill was doing well, its conifers dark against the bright sky. Smoke from burning rags or paper came from Bigbreck quarry. (Now who on earth would dump wooden boxes on a profitless quarry fire? - Someone whose house is all electric, of course!) White pylons shone up from a hilltop to the east, rising above the dark-topped plateau where the controversial peat-lands are.

Sweet-smelling grass fires scented the air, and blew in clouds across the road. Now the new greenery will get through without choking itself on the old. Swans were fending on a field near the Loch of Banks, and four wagtails flitted across a burn. A flock of small birds rose like a cloud, turning in unison to momentarily disappear, then materialise again, swooping and rising as an entity.

We returned to our abode with its lately land, where the daffodils were weeks behind those we had seen along the way. Larks sang, and snipe drummed; redshank, oystercatcher and curlew called. A lapwing cried "tee-veep, tee-veep," as ever her kind has done since my earliest days.

The Path through
The Woods

*T*hree little girls spent an evening here, playing out of doors in the twilight and by the bright light of the moon. Curious things happen when small feet race heedlessly over the moor; one came in to report: "I ran past a tree an' it jist fell doon!"

I can see that 'tree' from the window, leaning its leaves on the ground; it was a ridiculously tall piece of hedging which someone planted last year, and, although rooted, it had a poor grip of the earth.

One little girl stayed overnight, and, on Saturday, after a white night of frost, she asked, "Can we have a picnic, in the wood?"

The day was mild and springlike, as April ought to be. I packed egg sandwiches and plastic bottles of cold drinks, and we went down the road and through the iron gate. In the lee of our **17** hedge, daffodils danced in the breeze. A lark soared and sang. The whins, by our now overgrown well, were tawny-gold. Along the headrig of Binscarth's park, crimson-tipped daisies looked up with yellow eyes. The tracks of large birds overprinted tractor wheel-marks, and we saw a piece of rabbit fur, possibly the remains of a corbie's meal, or of my hunting cat's. Of late I have seen several rabbits playing in that field, their white tails bobbing.

The grass was gemmed with dew. A brig leading into the lower park makes a natural rockery. Gold moss spread fern-like fronds over stones; an exquisite small moss-cushion of light green grew beside another like a brown pincushion studded with spore capsules. The leaves of campion, nettle, dockan and dandelion were rising.

Hawthorn leaf-buds opened, although the gnarled branches wore more lichen than leaf. Under the hedge pink and white stars of claythonia opened beside the burnished yellow of celandine. Elder was in young leaf, but the beech still held last season's brittle old-gold. A rabbit, frozen with fright, sat pretending to be a stone with eyes; then, as we bent to touch it, became a white-tailed streak heading for the nearest burrow. Sheep clustered by their feeding trough; my companion found a pony to converse with across the fence. Bushes of snowberry lined a small enclosure below the brig, where two fields meet. Through this walled suntrap ran the burn, softly over flat brown stones, with the leaves of kingcup in the water's edge. One bush neatly filled a nook in the dyke, and there were mossy stepping stones by the steethe of the opposite wall.

The parasitic lichen has killed several hawthorns. This is a hoary, bearded type of lichen similar to that growing on standing stones and ancient dykes. (The variety now taking its living from my own small trees is flat and greeny-yellow.) They are vicious and insidious murderers, though they have a beauty of their own. I am inclined to blame these lichens for killing our native trees in the past.

Golden saxifrage, growing singly and looking like a dainty rarity, crept beneath the massed flowering currant that hung down from the low wall. Fuchsia was in leaf, and a carpet of celandine, wide awake in the sunshine, spread beneath the bare trees.

Wind soughed through the valley. Daffodils shone by the gate, and the garlic family was coming into flower. High in the tracery of branches against the sky, a fat, speckled thrush sang with all his might. Wood pigeons, handsome in blue and mauve, passed from tree to tree.

In the post-hurricane section of the plantation the young conifers have now reached a good height. There are several kinds of conifer here; and, as I am not versed in types of trees, I cannot give their correct names. Some of them are deciduous, so that a depth of fallen needles lie beneath them. One handsome, dark green fir which I always think of as the 'bottle brush tree' because of its round, thickly-needled branches, held little comes, as did several of the naked trees. A small cypress held its slender branches upward, in the shade of a conifer with blue-green needles. Holly and ivy shone; a wren called loudly as it flitted past.

A strange fungus, brown and shelving out from its host, grew on several trunks. Leaves of 19 the giant valerian rose along the verge, under a front of tall golden whin.

The air was soft and still; a bee sang by, and the wren now seemed to be scolding someone, with amazing volume for so small a body. Primroses opened, and the green rosettes of London pride stood shoulder to shoulder, promising a display of flowers later on. A dead tree-trunk had a covering of scale fungus which resembled shreds of bark. Dry, bleached leaves had worn away to a tracery of veins; leaf skeletons which we thought could be incorporated into a painting.

Ferns grew along the ridge of the dyke, and the burn ran slowly, brownly, to the sea. Through the gate we saw a pair of oystercatchers at home in the field, and my granddaughter thought we had come a long way, because Finstown appeared just ahead. "Can we have wir picnic noo?" she asked, and while I found a mossy stump to sit on she took off her coat and spread it on the grass. But very soon she shivered, got up and donned her coat again; and I became aware that a thermos of coffee would have been more appropriate to the day than bottles of orange.

There lay a fallen tree with its roots in the air. A primrose nestled in one root-hollow of a mossy stump, while a celandine looked brightly out from behind the next. These dead roots, taken over by a variety of smaller plants, are things of beauty. One, prone, with a cave beneath it, was clad in mosses of pale and dark green, liverwort, hard fern, St John's wort, and foxglove seedlings. A last year's fern hung long brown fronds down its side; and from the fern root rose the curled 'fiddle heads' of this season's growth, not yet unfurled. Our wren giving tongue, and, against a high cloud, three red-breasted birds swung on the top-most twigs overhead.

"There's a lovely silvery tree!" she said, admiring the smooth bark against the green.

"Here's someone's nest!" I said, pointing to a ball of moss firmly anchored in the pliant branches growing along its length and reaching straight upwards like new trees.

Of the trees felled by the hurricane that funnelled devastatingly through this valley twenty years ago, most have been removed, and the plantation has made a good recovery. some, their foundations badly shaken, have since developed a lean. Yet such is the innate vitality of trees that the roots are unwilling to die; one tree bole, looking rather like a toadstool, was apparently root-uppermost with its broken stump in the earth, but around it were numerous young branches rising tall and straight, bent on becoming a clump of tree. Another, with dried ferns growing out of it, had a sturdy sapling to either side. A fallen tree, a giant in our land, spanned the burn, its roots making an archway roofed with moss; and it, too, was alive in the secondary growth along its horizontal trunk.

Golden saxifrage grew everywhere, and much celandine gold. Liverwort clustered in close green scales, on stones and dead wood. Dried leaves moved on wind-currents as though of their own volition. An old nest, moss-made, occupied a crotch, and a spiderweb spanned last year's wren's nest in a hole in a long-dead stump. Another nest, from a former season, was constructed from heather twigs, and perched on a high bough.

A branch of hawthorn still held a few   21

berries. Through the trees, on the side of the hill, gleamed a yellow blaze of whin, behind which moved a flock of kye.

We shut the gate of the plantation behind us, and walked a short distance uphill. Dandelions shone, and honeysuckle clad the wall. Towards the northwest the trees decreased in height; we saw a weird, misshapen hawthorn, which hung all its branches downwards as though they had been discouraged at birth and bent against the wind. But flowering currant, in crimson glory, sheltered under a larger tree and flung its flowers forward across the ditch. In the light of noon the fields were very green, and rye grass was long enough to wave in the wind.

Once or twice in a year, perhaps, I take a walk along the right-of-way to Binscarth's plantation. There is always something new to see on that woodland path; and, enclosed by summer leaves, it holds a timeless peace.

The Shore of
the Harray Loch

"Six o'clock on Sunday morning is no time to discuss the weather," I said in answer to my man's comment on the "bonny morning". The sun beamed in from a clear sky and all the birds were in chorus. I went back to sleep.

Rising at what I considered to be a more reasonable hour, I watched a pair of little birds swing on a gooseberry branch. Their backs were brown with russet streaks, their tails, fronts, and heads dark grey with darker eye-streaks; they had sharp dark beaks and dark legs, and they were much less shy than the twites and reed-buntings that frequent the area. None of the illustrations in my books fitted their description, but that could have been due to the colour-reproduction, which has deceived me before. Midges danced in the sunlight, and a snipe soared to come rippling joyously down,

23

drumming in the spring. Larks sang, and one landed in the tattie-field.

Jim decided not to attend the Field Club outing, but Donnie came to the rescue and drove me to Bookan. Stenness was greener after the rain, and the fields were dancing with lambs. Celandines shone by Tormiston, and the lochs were blue.

Our party walked lochwards past massed daffodils that glowed golden under the hedge. The Wellington-booted bairns soon found an ipery ditch to splash in.

Drifts of the green velvety bobbles peculiar to the Harray Loch lay all the way along the shore. These are composed of algae, but look like small balls of moss. In the water's edge they swam on currents as though possessing motive power of their own, and once I came upon a patch of green algae not in ball formation idly swilling around in the ripples, as soft, disconnected mossy shreds.

A yowe butted her large lamb away; this was a pre-snow arrival, fat and sturdy. Marsh marigolds and celandines shone. Ducks circled and snipe drummed. Oystercatchers split the air with warning cries, raising every bird in the vicinity.

Bluebell, grape hyacinth and crocus leaves ran in a row along a bank where someone had planted them. On an area of short turf, among mosses of gold and green, we came upon a colony of vernal squill, not yet in flower, a long way from its usual habitat by the sea.

Geese had left their mark in the marsh we waded through. A pintail drake flew past. A lapwing's nest appeared, then two more were found by folk now treading warily, but the usually-vociferous owners were silent, demoralised by the approach of so many people.

We were in a bay, with offshore islands and reed-beds. Suddenly I remembered a sunny winter afternoon when I sat in the van, at the farm on the brae, overlooking this arm of the loch; now I had my bearings. A burn ran full of forget-me-not in young leaf. The reeds were as tall as a man, golden in the sunlight, and strong, fit for the Great God Pan. Iron-blue water ran in the bog. Horsetail raised soldier-like heads. Marsh cinquefoil, mint, bogbean and willowherb were small underfoot. A pale, spotted eggshell lay at my feet.

A flock of ducks passed. The sky, now smoky blue, was criss-crossed by cirrus; there were swirls, feathers, and layers of cloud, and, thinly drawn, the brilliant white trail of a high plane. Smoke followed us downhill from a straw fire. A few patches of snow still clung to the hillsides, and a soft purple horizon awaited evening. There were vole tracks in the wet grass, and a hare sat alert, watching us.

With sounding wing-slaps five swans rose, beating the water beyond the reeds. A mallard exploded from a rush-nest, and flew in a wide circle, leaving ten eggs in a feather bed. Numbers of teal swam in the distance, and coots paddled through the reeds. Snipe and whaups were plentiful, and a pair of ringed plover flew past. A couple of pintails sailed proudly on clear water.

The sunshine warmed the stones, and glinted on gossamers. We crossed a wide ditch by means of a brig, and watched the departure of half our company on their way home. Dabbling in the water, we caught small,

25

transparent freshwater shrimps, and saw sticklebacks dart away

A dyke stood with its feet in the loch, a broadly-built wall with its stones set on edge, typical of the Tenston district. Our youngest member found a little boat-house, apparently-built into the bank, and roofed with growing grass.

The way was long in the heat, and my face smarted with sunburn. We walked through the banked green algae drifts that lay, as soft as snow, along miles of shore, creamed over, here and there, with white froth churned by the waves.

Rounding a point, we walked over a field that smelt strongly of spring-time - a dung-spreader had been at work. Another, newly sown, lay smooth and finely tilled. In a bay was a chapel-site, and here we met the walkers who had started from the Mill of Rango. The party separated again, some going back to the mill to pick up transport and return to Bookan for the cars to collect the remainder of us. Beyond the chapel-site was a jutting headland, marked as a broch; but we went up the farm-road, and followed a long, winding way to the main road, past houses where daffodils waved, bairns played, and dogs came to see us. A wheatear darted from post to post; a rabbit, pop-eyed but pretending to be a stone, lost his nerve and bolted away with white tail bobbing. Kye in their byre bogled restively, scenting the fine spring air and longing for their green fields.

The temperature in the sunshine that morning had been in the seventies, and the soil temperature in the afternoon was 45 degrees. April was at her capricious best, and even the gossamers that festooned the day did not betoken worse weather to come, apart from mild rain and mist. Now the dew lies thickly, silvering the grass, and the air is full of music and wings.

From Yesnaby to the Bay of Skaill

At long last came a bright Sunday, with north-west wind and cold cloudbanks. A flock of swans fed at Brodgar, congregated where the fresh water runs through the brig; one was nesting in her accustomed place. A field near the stones has come under the plough; perhaps an archaeologist ought to be following the tractor. Mergansers dived in a blue pool, and on a golden islet gulls were nesting. Gold shone everywhere; dandelions blazed to challenge the kingcups. A boat of turquoise moved on the loch, under a blue broken sky. By the Yesnaby road a tortoise-shell huntress stalked through the reeds.

The sea sprayed thinly up the cliffs and the wind was wintry as the Field Club gathered; this is never a warm situation even on a summer's day. The sun struck through the rising waves, and clear greens rolled in, snow-crested; in geos where the foam swirled there frothed a blanket of creamy spume, washing to and fro like detergent suds or down at the edge of a duck-pond.

We examined the 'dyke' that runs up from the cliff edge; here were conglomerates, petrified pebble beds and the strange 'horse tooth' rock. This is a fascinating shore but one to be most happily visited when adventurous bairns are left at home, for sudden geos open and a gloup drops down to the sounding sea.

We found the primula scotica in its tiny purple brilliance, rising from the short turf; companioned by scurvy grass at ground level and the still-blind buds of squill. Close red buds of sea-pinks were beginning to open. The Broch of Borwick's lintel stone carried many names and initials; most of the party scrambled through the doorway to meet a draught of bitter wind. Fulmars sat on a ledge across the geo. A shower caught us by the sheep-dipping tank and we crept tight-packed under waterproofs while the rain streamed over our improvised tents.

Tesselated pavements, formed by successive mud-cracks in the days when the earth was new, still looked as though put together by the hand of man and carved for the floors of temples. The naked rocks, bared by gust and spray, lay in slabs of delicate colour and design, much more beautiful in their natural element than when transported elsewhere; a detached slab lying in my garden has lost its sea-washed freshness although it still resembles a sculptured female figure within a frame... suppose they were not created during the climatic and altitude changes of aeons when the basaltic ocean floor fluidly trembled, but that this portion of coast is a courtyard floor of Atlantis, and that dark dyke thrust up when the earthquake tore the land apart.... Oh, I know the theory of continental drift, and that America presumably stood just beyond our present shores; that the Atlantic continent, as it was then, vanished long before the coelacanths thought to try their limbs; and, in the billion years of change, these mud-flats rose and dried beneath a tropical heat, when fishes died on the broken, elevated lake-bottom which is now a layer of blue-grey stone.... Land masses drew apart, volcanoes rose, and no man was there to see; but life erupted within the mud, and we built ourselves with inexorable patience and purpose....

We came upon an egg a gull had stolen, a white shell irregularly blotched and yolk-stained. A long steep geo cut in, bird-whitened on its ledges. From a headland we saw the sea below draw back to make an onslaught on the craigs. It poured out of a cave, swirling as it receded around a pillar. Hoy's Old Man stood up clearly, and looking through binoculars at the Kame I saw a scooped-out slope angling down into the sea, as if an avalanche had fallen from the height of the hill; was this the scar of that landslide which precipated a portion of the cliff into the sea, so that clay-coloured water washed for years around its foot?

The nesting urge had taken possession of the kittiwakes, who came and went in waves, bringing in beakfuls of loch-bottom mud and weed to shape their nests. A firm fence came up; crawling under a loose wire, I arrived in a quagmire of clay; thick, sticky, scarcely wet, it sucked off my shoes to leave me discomfited in sock-feet. warmly yellow, it coated the retrieved shoes, and bound my now clay-soled socks more firmly into my lose footwear. These are unfortunate shoes; the first time they were worn

31

I was caught wet-footed by an advancing wave, and when my clothing begins its career by getting into trouble it has a habit of keeping it up.

Bairns ran along admiring violets, finding them too pretty to pick, learning lessons in beauty. On the eminence above Skaill we halted to eat lunch - my sandwiches were horrible, for which nobody was to blame but myself, and the coffee tasted of plastic beakers.

Out of a wind-funnelling geo came snow-balling spume, landing in silver and rainbow foam-crystals, quivering at my feet. Passing boots sprayed out salt drops from the drenched turf. More eggshells lay among the stones, including two pirated hen eggs, drained by the thieves. A shower drifted over us by the Hole o' Rowe. We went down-wind leaving a white cauldron of sea. A boat had come to anchor in the shelter of the bay. A few visitors walked around Skara Brae, and cars were among the dunes by the road. In the wall of the mill cheetered a bird's nest. The sea had encroached rapidly here, for at one time a cart-track ran between the mill and the shore, and enough grass grew there to pasture a tethered horse.

Here we met with more of our original party, including a woolly corgi puppy like a stub-tailed teddy bear. Slim terns flew overhead, on air-scything sickle-wings. The wind blew coldly as we waited for our returning transport and my damp feet grew heavy with chill; but much more than salt water would have been needed to damp the spirits of the younger generation. Walking along the edge of the tide, one young lady was caught unawares by a rising wave which soaked her from the seat downwards and filled her boots with sea-water, which disaster she greeted with hilarity as she skipped around bare-footed.

Our long-tailed ducks were still in residence on the Loch of Skaill, and golden-eye paddled by the road. The daffodils along the banks had faded dark-yellow, and primroses were at the height of their bloom. The wind died quietly away, leaving a bird-filled evening deeply blue.

Westray in June

"Isles trips," declared my man, "are for fine days only! If there's wan drop o' rain on Thursday morning we're no gaun!"

"If we wait for weather in Orkney," I said, "we'll never get anywhere. The only thing is tae go, regardless o' weather!"

This is a precept I seldom follow, nevertheless, for gales discourage me all too easily. But Thursday dawned fair and light of wind, after a quiet night when we lay ringed in a frosty mist which breathed up out of the swamp. The shy was blue, the early forecast good, and the air full of birdsong.

Kirkwall pier had become a parking place. People thronged the space between the stores and the North Isles boats. Aboard the "Sigurd" I leaned against the warm funnel and watched the *Orcadia* move smoothly out behind us, steal

35

swiftly past and proceed with ease into the distance, while we headed more slowly into the tide and wind.

The *Orcadia* passed between Vasa Skerry and the shore of Shapinsay, her masts appearing above the Grass Holm. Balfour Castle rose above the trees. Terns and gulls, and a plume of black reek, followed us. Kirkwall became small and low, with the Cathedral in its heart.

Rousay's fields were snowed over with daisies. veronica edged the shore with purple flowers, and houses grew green with ivy. The deep water boiled up, ice-green, as we winched slowly in to the pier. Rousay has changed since I saw it last, for electric cables span the island.

Egilsay pier was a peninsula on a narrow isthmus of road. St Magnus Kirk towered up, a dominating landmark. Small waves danced on the rising swell, and the sunlight bounced back off the sea. There was a great deal of sea between Rousay and Rapness, but the swell increased as we sailed towards Papa Westray, until, in sheltered water again, we met the little blue motor boat which had come to collect the Papa Westray contingent. We could see the new pier, and the beach of snow-white sand; beneath us was green water above a sandy floor. Terns, dunter drakes, and puffins flew past.

Neat sheaves of dried tangles were stacked on Gill Pier. Yachts rode at anchor in the harbour as we walked towards Pierowall. The island was as beautiful as I remembered it from former visits; there was the well with the steps leading up to the pump, the flag-roofed houses, and the sandy fields. Potatoes and cabbages throve in the soft clean earth. The old roof-fallen kirk lifted one gable end and four walls, among the grave-stones that rose from uneven ground mounded up in one corner. The sand has not migrated from this sheltered bay in the winter storms, although the west coast bays of the Mainland and Hoy have lost their sand.

Pasture was daisy-white and scanty of grass, but the summer voices of corncrakes sounded all around. We walked past the school and towards Noltland. A ringed plover pursued a blackbird from its territory among the oats; presently we saw the other little anxious parent, and then their family came into view running swiftly, shepherded between the pair. A huge bee bumbled among the flowers, but of the golden dandelions only ghosts remained, from which streamed tiny parachutes down the wind.

In the bush roadside grass shone double buttercups as handsome as garden flowers, and on the links football pitch were drifts of daisies so intensely white that they hurt the eyes. The gull flock sitting ashore nearby were dull by comparison. A dog wagged up to us. Snowy white washing flew on the fresh breeze.

At Noltland the already tidy lawn was being cut by a motor mower. Not a blade of grass escaped attention. This is a windy castle, and full of echoes, but the sun beat down in the courtyard where we sat on wall-foundations to eat a picnic lunch. Flies sang around us, attracted by the empty cups, and pigeons were in residence. Cameras clicked; folk came and went. We were a party of five basking in the sun, and wandering into the cool dark halls of the Castle and up the wide stone stairs, blinded by the sudden transition from brilliant light to darkness.

I went half way up, then down again to the ground floor. There is something eerie in that cold dim place with its high arched roof, lit only

37

by gunports. Jim searched for masons' marks on the stones, finding some to correspond with those of the Earl's Palace in Birsay. In the great fireplace a red, velvety fungus crept over the stones where the fire had been. I could not look over the edge when we climbed to the top of the stairs, but leaned against the wall while the wind cried over the heights.

The building has an air of durability with its great square stone blocks, and thick walls built to withstand a siege, but whose are the bones heaped beneath the mound in the north-east corner?

When the Ministry of Works took over Noltland they intended levelling that mound, to make a flat park around the castle. But bones came to light, and cloven skulls, all of mighty men, heaped in a vast communal grave. The excavations were halted and the mound remained, a green, smooth elevation.

Leaving Noltland we obtained a lift in a car to Rackwick where our company divided at the cottage with the sundial in its yard. Jim and I walked to the shore where multitudinous tangles hung drying on long dykes. Here I met bulbous buttercup, a plant for which I searched for years until I began running into it all over the county. On the shore were logs such as have been coming in around our coasts for some time, grown over with barnacles and worm-bored to the heart, telling of long journeyings.

We climbed dykes, walked past Trenabie, and came to the Ouse where the sand lay dry. Ringed plovers were plentiful, and shelducks probed the sand. The sun beamed down, but feathers of cirrus were overhead.

Corncrakes called as we walked back to the pier, past flag-roofed houses and daisied land.

On the low shore, to the east of the bay, fulmars nested. One took wing, leaving her white egg revealed. Under a cave-roof formed by a rockfall, a nest of starlings cheetered.

The swell of the morning had eased, and the homeward trip was quiet. I watched the slanting cliffs of Rapness pass, cave-cut and inhospitable, with seas breaking white at their feet. Puffins and terns flew around us.

Faray lay dark and unpeopled, its stone houses at the mercy of winds, birds and sheep. Rousay approached, across a silver-grey sea where ripples broke.

A colder air came out of the west, and we retreated below into the warmth until Kirkwall pier drew up to welcome us.

A Day Across
The Firth

Just before the anti-cyclone left us, we got a Saturday evening phone call. Were we interested in a fine-weather Sunday trip across the Pentland? My man said "yes" forthwith, although I cast a wary eye to the sky, anticipating a change.

Morning brought a long bank of mist which lay blackly over Orphir and greyly over Hoy. The wind was still. We drove past golden buttercup banks, and spires of purple orchids; yellow mosses, tawny whins, black and white kye, hayfields with a sheen of purple and silver, and sea-sand-green silage stubble. The sky was clear to the north where the isles lay in sunlight, but the Flow was pearl-grey under cloud.

Bird's foot trefoil clad the verges in sheets of flame-colour. A swan was nesting by St Mary's Loch. Now the Orphir hills were dark behind us, 41 and the long, pale Hoy-line stretched to west-ward. Turnips grew in red earth at Herston; huge crimson garden poppies hung their heads. Ponies grazed by the mill, and the burn ran through a forest of segs, marsh marigold and wild parsley. The flowers, I noted, were ahead of ours; we are only a few miles nearer to the North Pole, but it shows!

Pleasantly situated along the lee side of Widewall Bay, the Herston village faces several roofless crofts across the water, and Roeberry House standing tall on the brae. The broch and headland of Hoxa lie to the north. The Swona boat, with tall mast, lay at anchor, for the pier was high and dry in a very low ebb. I walked along the shore, collecting bonny stones, which I stowed in the boot of the car.

The pier was weed-slippery. Brown, green, and fern-fronded seaweeds edged the sea, and sea-slugs lay on the sand; weird beasts, with four horns, that sprouted purple dye when picked up. I wore a pair of thigh-length fisherman's boots to board the dinghy which ferried us out to the larger boat; the boots went over my shoes.

We moved smoothly out past creels with plastic bottle floats and composition corks. Stanger Head rose opposite Hoxa, their twin batteries a reminder of days when little pleasure attended Pentland crossings and sailings in the Flow. Cantick Lighthouse came into view, and the Martello tower at Longhope. Impressive cliff architecture rose as we rounded Herston Head, sea-sculptured into caves and arches, white washed by seabirds. Red craigs curved in to Sandwick.

Swona, home of our boatman and his boat, shouldered up from the tide. Ships passed through the Firth. Scotland lay palely to the south. We ran with never a wave, except our wake, in sight; the sea was oily black, blue shadowed, and glittering with sunlight. Puffins used their wings as paddles. Guillemots paid us no heed. A solan winged past. South Ronaldsay's western bulwark, Barth Head, stood squarely in the waveless swell now lifting the boat. The Pentland Skerries, twin towered, had shrugged off the morning mist. We were bathed in sunlight, but cooled by ocean air.

South Ronaldsay slanted down to a low ness; a beacon stood on a skerry. No one would have believed, on such a shining day, that the gentle sea that buoyed us up could ever be a ship-swallower and destroyer of men.

Ships roamed the sea-road. We passed Stroma, very obviously an unpeopled island. Flat swirls of water sucked at the boat; but whirlpools, like lily pads with dimples in their hearts, do not menace motor boats these days.

Arriving at John O'Groats we found the tide still low. An iron ladder, built into the pier, was our only means of access into Scotland.

This northern outpost is tourist conscious. A seaside stall sold souvenirs and guidebooks — the shell ornaments, bracelets and necklaces, were very attractive, and shell-covered boxes, a revival of an old art, were beautiful indeed. But we were reminded forcibly that Orkney is not part of Scotland. The cottage on the windswept shore advertised itself as "the last house in Scotland", postcards and placards said so, as if the Pentland had not already assured us of the fact. John O'Groats and Duncansby Head, across the powerful, pulling tide, are, entirely apart from advertising, very much the top of the map.

Orkney and Shetland are places with a   43

character of their own. Withdrawn behind the unpredictable sea, pushed by cartographers into spare corners of the Scottish sheet, they are by no means only bits left over from the making of the British Isles. Remote from the Sooth we may be; we are also protected from the rush and bustle of cities, and to us these are remote.

Along the shore that tops the map of Scotland we found shell sand; but I carried home a hankyful of yellow winkles which now repose in a jam dish. They range from just off-white through pale lemon to deep orange. Green ones, and striped ones, complete the colour range. Their colours are brighter than those gathered at the Brough of Birsay in the spring.

Tourists were out in force, along the shore, on the clifftops, and on the road leading to Duncansby Head Lighthouse. The sun beat down as we rounded the Ness of Duncansby and climbed towards the headland. Bulbous buttercups shone all the way, and adder's tongue fern grew in a short turf.

A steep-sided, deep gloup opened on Duncansby Head, walled with sheer rock on one side, and echoing with the voices of birds. On its sunward side grew vivid red campion, sea-pinks, primroses, heather, meadowsweet, and scurvygrass.

The Caithness orchids were ahead of ours, the heath-spotted variety already browning at the edges whereas their Orcadian counter parts were newly blown. Moonwort ferns grew on the headland, larger than ours; along with the scillas, marsh violets, tormentil, trefoil, heath bedstraw, cotton grass, and lady's smock.

A steep geo by the lighthouse resembled the Gloup; gulls and puffins occupied its ledges.

Here we met a friendly English couple, bound for Orkney the following day; their last year's holiday had been postponed because of the seamen's strike. "And where do you come from?" he inquired.

White, sun-bright sand lay in the Bay of Sannick, with rock ridges running out like furrows. The road swept across the moor; Orkney lay out to sea. "We cam' fae ower the water jist for the day," I answered.

Sunset in the Sea

We saw the hump of Copinsay to the north-east as we stood on the headland of Duncansby. The sun poured down; a strong tide ran through the Firth. Westward rose Dunnet Head. One of these Big Hooses, we thought, must be the Castle of Mey, but a slight haze shadowed the land and visibility was poor.

Beyond the lighthouse and over the brae was another deep slanting geo, in land that glowed rose pink with thrift. The headland and seaward side of the geo wore tightly packed cushions of sea-pink, ranging from deep rose to very pale pink, and brightened by red campion. Sea campion and marguerites shone whiter than the gulls crying overhead. Lovage was not yet in flower. Guillemots, fulmars, hoodie crows and pigeons sat on ledges or rode air currents far below, their calls echoing in the confines of the chasm.

47

The stacks of Duncansby rose ahead of us; unlike any of our rock castles, they are broad-based and tapering towards the top, pinnacled as if carefully pared down. All around that shore creel-floats were visible, even between the stacks. The remains of a trawler raised a rusty projection, like a periscope, close below the cliff. Out to sea, a large ship bore northwards.

The stacks come out of clear water; two tall, one small, another in process of breakaway from the parent craig. A climber had attached a small flag to the highest pinnacle; no mean feat, because the rock appeared to be crumbly, part of the slope being scree rather than solid stone.

A family of young jackdaws fluttered out of the cliff-face. We found a corner-post of the fence picturesquely embedded in shell-sand concrete. A fenced clifftop is less awe-inspiring than an open one; I could look over the edge without that expectation of falling which always alarms me at home.

Underfoot were kidney vetch, milkwort, eye-bright, ribwort, buckshorn and sea-plantains, crowberry, and the glittering gold of tormentil. Peatbanks stretched inland, with good black peat. We sat down on a bank to have a picnic meal, but were driven back to the edge of the cliff by hordes of hungry midges. A sea-breeze funnelling up a geo blew them back to the heather. I must state that the Scottish midges are much more voracious than ours; and Orkney midges can be savage enough to spoil any fine evening.

Walking back across the moor we watched the clouds gather. The peatbanks were dry-footed, and the Caithness tuskar, unlike ours, is a one-man implement. Goldenrod grew every-where, and two plants, carefully dug up, came home with me in the lunch-box.

We arrived on the Lighthouse road again after crossing a field of rushes. Huge crimson orchids grew by the road. Oatfields were patchy, as if "grub" had been active; this seems to be a leather-jacket year, for every spade of turned earth in our plots held these grubs.

Scotland, to me as to many travellers, means mountains, rocky outcrops, and harebells. At the cost of a car-hire we could have had these, but chose instead to explore this bit of coastline on foot. On holiday, in the past, we often intended to tour slowly through the wild scenery of the north and west, leaving the car long enough to walk mountain tracks and get the atmosphere of the place; yet the open road always tended to lead us farther south, and the days were not long enough for all that we had planned. I came back to John O'Groats, after our big day, vaguely disappointed in not having seen a mountain, nor a dancing harebell, nor a lilied lochan black-watered in the hills.

But the sea was glorious, that lifting surging Firth, holding back its waves until we were safely home. We left the pier at 9 o'clock, while the tide still ran, and under the black western cloud a long low yellow horizon lay. The sun was still high; a white ball burning through the cloud.

We drove out towards Stroma, lying lifeless offshore: another island where a pier was built in time to let the inhabitants depart! There was a good enclosed harbour, a safe anchorage against the ocean swells. Many solidly built homes stared blankly out to sea. An old kirkyard on a eastern headland had the remains of a square-built monastery still standing, with large corner-stones like those of Noltland Castle and the Egilsay Kirk.

49

Church and school stood on the face of the brae. The rock-strata dipped towards the sea. We headed for Swona, across smooth lifts of tide. Hoy lay empurpled, with translucent sheen of rose-red; an enchanted isle that would at any moment change. Under the low sun, the sea was shot with gold and silver to the west, but when I looked to the eastward I saw the sunset deep within the sea. Over the boat's side the water was clear to the depths, and through it ran all the colours of the spectrum — violet, blue, purple, old-gold, rose, and green. These shades did not only overlie the surface; they filled the sea, and with every slow swell they moved in curls and swirls.

I am a sea-watcher, who must anticipate every motion of wave and tide lest they catch me unawares. But also I look out hopefully for sea-beasts, known and unknown; for who can tell when a plesiosaur of the Loch Ness type may come dripping up from below or a whale or porpoise surface? There are strange creatures in the sea, from phosphorescent animalculae to weed-grown monsters yet un-named.

Rows of birds were barnacled to the cliffs of Swona, and puffins met us. The sunset faded, and the luminescence dulled to grey. Below the cliffs of South Ronaldsay two otters appeared shining sleekly as they ran from the water and out of sight. The sky and sea shone brightly; white towers of cloud rose among grey, and the water was marbled black and white. A weather change was on the way.

Swimming by the barriers were two more otters, their black heads, backs and tails visible, trailing little V wakes behind them. I wished them well, and hoped no gunman came their way. Nearing midnight, in the midsummer season, we arrived home, still feeling the glow of that sun on the afternoon sea, now that the car heater had warmed us after the return voyage. A few years ago I was very wary of crossing large seas in peedie boats; but now I have developed a taste for such trips, at least in fine weather.

A Visit to Hellyar Holm

We could use more fine summer Sundays than one year is likely to provide, exploring the more accessible of our smaller isles.

Those which may be reached by open boat require carefully chosen occasions of calmly polished seas, or of sun-blue ripples, before I can be persuaded to embark. To move over translucent water, where every stone and weed-frond is visible and sea-urchins crawl spikily on the bottom, is pleasant indeed; to pass through a shoal of small pulsating jellyfish or flickering finger-sized sillocks leaves a shining photo-graphic memory. To set foot on a hitherto unvisited shore is always an adventure.

It is more than thirty years since my first visit to Hellyar Holm, and the schoolboy who rowed us across the quiet Bay of Elwick is many years dead. Of that outing I remember little

53

except the clinical cleanness of the lighthouse; the steep stair and the burnished brass; the catwalk outside the lantern where we looked across the String towards the beacon on the Head of Work; the sundial in the yard; and the live pull of the sea against me as I tried my hand at the oars on our way home.

When I was a bairn Hellyar Holm lay between us and the sunset, rising darkly in front of Wideford Hill. On the shortest day the sun set directly over the tower on the Holm when viewed from our door. I knew that this isle, like most of the holms throughout Orkney, had at one time its monastery or chapel, reputedly a retreat of the Culdees. This is marked on the large Ordnance Survey map as sited on its north-east shore.

The reef, making of Hellyar Holm a peninsula at extreme low tide, reached out to join Shapinsay beyond Liviness Geo. Anyone attempting to cross this causeway on foot had to leap the central channel; perhaps these "anchorites and scribes" from the hermitage walked through this very ebb to minister to the pre-Viking people of the larger island....

A week ago a party of us left Kirkwall by motor boat to spend an afternoon on Hellyar Holm. It was a cool grey day with north wind. We sailed at low water to land at the lighthouse pier. With an inshore wind the waves break high on this point, but the pier shelters in a little harbour formed by a natural breakwater, where a ridge of rock juts out into the tideway.

We found a whitewashed concrete path leading towards the lighthouse, so snowy that to walk on it seemed a desecration. The head lightkeeper came to meet us, and kindly conducted us through the tower, explaining how the apparatus worked.

How immaculately brilliant lighthouses rise! The brasses shone as I remembered them, the clock ticked slowly, and the stairs ascended steeply. Three flights led us to the light itself, a mantle which becomes incandescent on the principle of a tilley lamp and is magnified enormously by an ingenious arrangement of hundreds of prisms, which multiply that seemingly tiny lightsource into great ship-warning beams.

We glanced at the sundial as we left the buildings; it was timeless through lack of sun. Rocks rose on edge along the shore, tystes dived and swam with delightfully crimson paddle feet, a rock pipit chirped shrilly, and a lark sang. In a burrow we found a tyste's nest with two speckled eggs.

The depressions of kelp holes were green on the banks. Scillas starred the turf, scurvy grass and pinks grew in scant root-hold. Sorrel, blinks, bedstraw, tormentil, buttercup, spearwort and bird's foot trefoil we noted, and violets of the deepest blue that I have ever seen, finely white-veined. Tall, handsome thistles, spear and marsh varieties, were in bud. Lady's smock and marsh marigold ran along a damp ditch.

The walls of the old fish-curing station were in good repair, with rafters still intact although fallen slates strewed the floor. Nettles throve there, those camp-followers and survivors of man's passing. A brackish pool, sun-sucked so that its floating covering of green weed had dried, bleached, and sunk as ice does in a thaw, was situated behind an ayre. Silverweed and creeping buttercup carpeted the stones, pearlwort grew in mossy cushions, plantain and sea purslane bordered the pool. Wild iris, marsh dandelion, and curled dock kept company with several species of rushy and sedgy things, and grasses in bloom. The short grass was dotted with daises, and clovers red and white.

At the end of a reef a pillar had been built, part of it at least of recent construction because it wore a large black tyre around its shoulders. We found traces of building along the east coast, one site evidently that of a broch and another apparently a sheepfold, with aged, hoary lichen upon its stones. Where is the chapel-site? Has it been adapted to form that sheep-shelter or has it grown over with grass? There is a Kirk Geo marked on my small map.

Somewhere on the short turf grew a little plant, chickweed wintergreen, quite a rarity in Orkney.

A blackbird, querulously conversational, kept an eye on us; a few terns swooped, but the expected colony was not in evidence. Oyster-catchers' cries jarred the air, and a few very angry gulls swept our heads with the wind of their wings. Fulmars glided, and sat cosily on ledge nests. The bones of a gone gannet had settled among the shore stones; a dunter's nest was cold and deserted, its down scattered as if the duck had vacated it hastily, never to return.

Here was a flat-rocked shore, gradually rising to cliffs that were less high than I had thought. Rocks wore flat yellow lichen and tufted grey, with dark lumps of moss. Sea campion clung in crevices. The sea sounded underfoot, lazily swelling through a rock bridge.

Spotted orchids rose from the heath, where the heather was short and the sea-gusted blaeberry and crowberry grew in abundance, though no berries were as yet visible. Many of the deep blue violets grew by the central tower.

A looper caterpillar hunched its way over a raised stone slab. Rusty brown fungoid growths, not mushrooms, had an unhealthy appearance. Two kinds of cotton grass, silken soft, blew gently on the breeze.

A steep geo cut into the south-east corner, with clean-washed slanting strata. Here the clifftop was as bare as that of Yesnaby; this headland takes the force of the swells and gales coming up the String. Pinks, tenaciously rooted, flourished everywhere. A flock of skarfs rose and fell on the moving sea.

Across the water the Head of Work beacon stood four-square, that erection which, in my infant years, appeared as a bending giant docking turnips on an island situated far beyond my world. I am still sad to lose illusions and solve mysteries, for youth and wonder vanish when things have been explained. He is a big tarry monster, this giant, patiently standing there as a mark for shipping to loom out of the fog, perhaps, on an occasion when headlands are not easily distinguishable and a vessel might 'mis-marrow' them and run ashore. Just such an accident almost happened once, disaster being averted by a fisherman's timely shout, but that is a story for another day....

The evening had mellowed by departure-time. We ate a picnic tea along with curious flies which persisted in drowning in our coffee. One beautiful crimson orchid stood to advantage on the cliff, and brown, hair-like weed waved softly on the sea-floor as we sailed away.

A Walk to
the Hamars

"My, that's a wintry soond," a visitor remarked as the gale came snarling around the end of the house, one evening shortly after midsummer. The turn of the days came imperceptibly, bringing no fine weather, and the midnight sun made its small circling of the North obscured in heavy cloud; the book I took out of doors at one o'clock could have been read, but not for pleasure. As someone pointed out to me, the weather is at least consistent and predictable; we know by this time what to expect.

Now, in the early days of July, spates and autumn-sounding winds strike an ominous note, because these are the conditions commonly associated with Lammas-time; the season is still a month ahead of schedule, and the early-opening flowers were not so much anticipating summer as snatching at the offered sunshine while they could. When we see the sun its light is brilliant, but it has a hard quality due to the tempering northerly winds.

We cut a belated peatbank on the last Saturday of June. Our fuel is at varying stages, half of it long overdue for carting. This final cutting was bottom peat, bedded on clay; which came up on long black slabs where it was not tree-broken. With some difficulty a large root was levered out, a primeval hazel surrounded by its nut-shells. Deep down, the peat was pale amber and of a mossy texture. This layer had an ancient odour, and the cold of centuries struck my boots and gloves.

"They'll never dry," John prophesied. "Peats should be cut before June."

A new farm road is branching out, and the existing track over which we have driven so often now has an even base; gone are the deep ruts and mud holes we splashed and lurched through in the spring. Right in the digger's path a few fragrant orchids rose, all innocent of their fate; we halted, and with a pocket knife and fingers probed down to dig them up. I planted them on my heathery lupin brae.

The sun blazed through a cooling westerly wind. We arrived home just as the phone rang to arrange a long-promised trip to the Hamars that afternoon.

Syradale has an air all of its own, appreciably milder than that of the open plain, except when a wind is funnelling up the valley. The west wind and a haze of cloud followed us. Wild pansies edged a field where cattle grazed; we passed another dressed in pink and gold, where ragged robin spread a close carpet of colour on one side and buttercups, in an extravagance of burnished yellow, lit the other half. Crossing the firm fence which divides the cultivation from the hill we found wild roses and ferns in the bed of a dry burn. Spider-webbed hollows made tiny traps in the damp turf. On the burnt hillside bracken rose in a pale green wave.

The fuchsia which runs down the Hamars increases yearly. Dripping with blossom, it hung in a canopy over the burn. The waterfall sprayed out from moss-brown rocks, singing in the shelter; ivy leaves shone and nettles stood guard, but a large heather-and-twig-built nest had been cast down into the burn. Rock faces wore generations of initials; a natural rockery crept, rooted in crevices; maidenhair, spleenwort, mountain willowherb, golden saxifrage, and that small, proudly branching plant which stands on the edge of a quite-inaccessible crag.

I can recall a March excursion to the Hamars of Syradale a good many years ago, when I found two-feet-long icicles in the burn, a sheeted waterfall, several robins, and a restless flashing brilliancy of migratory goldcrests in the leafless fuchsia. That day I sat entranced for an hour on a stone; such scenes come but seldom.

This summer day, in the shelter of an ivied overhang, a banded snail crept, drawing in its head at an approaching finger but presently extending its neck again, and warily waving its horns.

Bright pink and rose-like, a freak water avens appeared underfoot. This specimen's petals were held upright, making of that habitually head-hanging and modest plant a flower to grace a garden; yet, if transplanted into a flower-bed, such mutations will bloom normally the next season.

Going farther up the valley we were pushed by the strengthening wind which had become trapped between the hills and was hastening to pour out over the plateau above. On the level hilltop half a gale blew. A West Mainland panorama stretched all around. Pale silver sea shone over Sandwick, and Hoy rose clearly above the Sound. Wideford Hill was spiked with matchsticks and Kirkwall clustered in its lee. Hellyar Holm Lighthouse gleamed white, Shapinsay was low and mistily green with the Castle rising from its dark pewter-coloured sea. Cattle gazed at us over a fence; we had reached the Rendall side of the hill.

A peat road led back to the upper reaches of the Syradale burn, where the fuchsias were not so tall; here, a year ago, we had seen a wood pigeon's nest with its curious, vulture-like, half-fledged young. The hill dropped away alarmingly as we descended; the valley was wet-footed but pleasant to walk through because the July jungle was only beginning to rise. June is the most beautiful summer month, when low flowers colour the land before the rank vegetation takes over.

A rain-cloud broke as we reached the fields. The opulent purple orchids lining the roadway stood clean-washed, and the grass-blades shook themselves dry, as the shower took to the hills and we trod the hard road home.

The West in Wind and Sun

Swans were arched and sailing along the Stenness Loch edge, and fishers encamped on the Harray shore as we drove west. Many ducks and coots dabbled in the valley pools along the Yesnaby road, and clean pigs trotted on free range, one ambling in front of the car.

A brightness hung in the air but the wind blew bitterly, and blue-white heaps of sea moved below the craigs. In the windy, close-grown turf gleamed the primula scotica; we searched each patch of purple for its vivid colour, more royal than the tints of thyme and self-heal appearing stemless in carpet-pile grass. One proud cluster stood match-tall, blowing in the sea-breeze, and this our friend recorded on his colour-film, while my man acted as a wind-break; but still the little stem bent and wavered in eddying gusts, and another was eventually found with a briefer

63

stem, which stood still to be photographed.
Trefoil made a perfect contrast, and a miniature
bush of eyebright added variety.

Fewer folk were abroad than usual, the west
craigs being at least a coat colder than inland.
The herons were too far away to visit on an arctic
day, but we made plans for another occasion.

Said someone on that drenching Saturday
of Shopping Week, while we sought shelter from
the rain: "Surely your man has a lot o' days off
afore you can go aboot so much?"

Such a misapprehension I must
immediately correct; this man of mine has no
day off except Sunday, and the Hoy week-end
was his first holiday in three years. On week-day
roamings I am either solitary or accompanied by
companions with similar interests. My latest
outing took me along the west craigs from
Yesnaby to Stromness, just three days after our
chilly Sunday trip, on a sultry day fleeced with
cloud of silver white, while thunder-heads of
inky black rolled and changed to the eastward
but did not break. This was a sudden
resurgence of summer, in colours intense as
technicolor; Mediterranean blue sea, and sky
borrowed from remembered years. Primulas
gemmed the turf in places where I had not
previously seen them; and somewhere along
that enchanted coast we found an orchid of
unobtrusive but rare beauty, to be admired and
photographed. It rose compactly out of broad-
based, ground-level, short and tapered leaves;
its florets were distinctly hooded above a strap-
shaped tongue, and of a purple-yellow tone. In
the large view-finder it was a lovely thing. Later,
consulting all the botanical books we had left
behind, we concluded that it could only be a frog

orchid, although the flower-spike was shorter and denser than the only illustration I could find; but this could have been the result of environment.

The headlands in front shaded out from brown and green into dark blue, culminating in the clear blue of Hoy with the Old Man standing boldly; along the horizon reached the nebulous shape of the Scottish coastline, and far to the west lay a golden streak between sea and sky. Several fishing-boats were out; the sea was still, except for a slow slight swell sighing against the craigs, occasionally breaking hollowly into caves. Of the three rock stacks, those of North Gaulton are more spectacular than the better-known Castle of Yesnaby. One of these rises erect from a narrowed base in the centre of a geo, and nearby, at a respectful distance from the edge of the shore, we rested to picnic on sandwiches and Ferguzade from a plastic bottle. During our walk this container had changed its shape, now having its sides swollen like a horse with colic; an air-space occupied the top, due to the effervescence in the drink. It was refreshing and sweet, but I was sleepy; the sun beat down, and when I closed my eyes I could see the brilliant orange negative image of the sea. "I'll get sunstroke," I declared, "an' after the coldest summer on record, that would go down in history!"

Mackerel trails were in the sea, and along this stretch of oily calm I saw momentary black streaks rise and go down again; either the glistening dark bodies of the fish themselves, or something preying upon them. Far out a fishing-boat was gutting fish, for a snow-shower of gulls had descended on his wake. We had missed the heronry, having gone past before

65

recognising Lyra Geo, but two herons flappedgreat wings with deceptive slowness across a geo farther on. Along Mousland a sheep stared at us and moved out of our way. Here we found a devourer devoured: the body of a black-back which had been partially eaten.

Two burns came out of the hills, burns with dark pebble beds where some have found the glint of gold, for a vein of yellow metal runs somewhere through that brooding land. Out here, I often think, there is room for an entire small community, and here, if I ever write that authentic Orkney tale as I have threatened to do, I will set my scene.

"That's the Black Craig," we said, as the half-sea-fallen hill rose before us, with its look-out post facing the Atlantic. Underfoot was turf less springy than the close-cushioned thrift we had trod before; here rose a perfect wheel of marguerites, fern-foliage-spoked into the centre, every flower immaculate.

"Grass of Parnassus? No!" We stopped to examine a plant. "I think we've got something!" I said. The flower standing sturdily at our feet had a square, substantial, ridged stem, typically veined petals but with sepals longer than the petals, and the wrong leaf; this clasped the stem firmly with a very broad base and was twice as long as the normal one. But more Grass of Parnassus grew nearby, and we were forced to conclude that our plant was a freak. Neverthe-less, it asked to be photographed.

Through thistled grass we walked uphill, finding a track leading eventually to the Strom-ness road. But while the clifftops had not wearied us, we found the road hard going under the merciless sun; turning my reversible jacket white-side out relieved me only slightly, and we were glad of a lift for the last long half-mile.

"My, you've got the sun," they said.

Later that evening came a phone call. "Are you coman oot tae the cuithes?"

I roused my sleeper out of the chair where he was relaxing, and we got ready for the sea, only to find no car. I snatched up the phone again, but our fishers had left for the shore.

"We'll tak the van," I suggested.

"Oh no, we won't," he said firmly.

We called our elder son a few names not usually cast in his direction, for the car could be anywhere in the West Mainland and we were holding up the fishing on an ideal evening.

"I ken whar he is!" I exclaimed suddenly. "On the loch!"

"Yes, an' I can see him fae here - awey at the opposite side o' the water!"

Our car was three miles away; we made another phone call. "Please see if you can find that boy an' send him home immediately!" But one cannot communicate with a boat in the middle of a loch, and our son found a large grocery van in place of the car on his eventual return to shore.

We had lost half an hour and the sun had set. All the pools were smoking after the day's heat, and white curls of mist streamed over low fields. A bank of solid blue cloud, with rising pillars, reached out above rose pink. The Bay of Skaill shone glass-green, the loch held the house mirrored on pink and blue, tern wings beat doubled in air and water. Dragon cattle breathed smoke in two spreading plumes. A flat white sea reached out to America.

67

The black memorial rose on Marwick Head; the horizon lay in sunset colours as we drove down to the shore. The men hauled the boat into a low tide, and we rowed out upon a wide purple sea.

Swells were long and slow; I saw them come, but the motion was scarcely perceptible. I have a fear of small boats because of the nearness of the water; also, this one had a list towards the side my man occupied.

"You couldno' get a better night," they assured me, and beyond Marwick Head our companion boat moved smoothly into the sunset; we could see a figure hauling fish, and presently the wand I was awkwardly holding moved in my hand. I had to wait for my man to remove the cuithe from the hook; around our feet flapped sleek cold bodies drowning in air.

The water held passing circlets of gold; the craigs were awesome above us, cave-cut and overhanging. Roosting seabirds on their lime-washed rocks called like hens disturbed at bedtime; the sea sounded in blue-floored caves. To the east rose a great round light; it was Jupiter, but seeming so huge that I thought it to be some unchancy thing sent up from earth. Far to the west passed little lights on the horizon, as the fishing-boats we had watched that afternoon went down with their catch to Scrabster.

"You gettan many?" our two row-boats spoke each other as we rounded Marwick Head. The top of the memorial rose like a castle turret; north of us blinked the Brough Lighthouse.

"No; we'd better go home." We turned down-tide and the sea followed us back to the Noust. Jupiter had climbed high, a great gold lantern over Howe. Getting me ashore proved more difficult than anticipated and I almost took two unwary brothers-in-law overboard into cold black sea, while my man laughed.

We ate fried cuithes at midnight, and dawn was reaching up the sky as we drove home. Through the Marwick valley and along the Twatt road lay a lake of white vapour, and above the hill rose a strange cloud-mirage of buildings in a deep-blue land; and after that wonderful day I was prepared to accept it as such, an image of Norway brought over by the dawn. All the next day I experienced a mild heaving sensation, as if my being still moved gently upon a swelling sunset sea.

Summer
Days in Sanday

I have always thought of mists as slightly
magical, by their knack of concealing land-
marks and making familiar places into
unknown lands. But a mist spoiled our view of
Sanday's unique coastline as seen from the sea;
for the houses come up like a mirage before
there is any sign of land. This was my first visit
to the island; and now we were at large there,
still enclosed by grey vapour. Having made no
plans beforehand, we set out on foot, with the
aid of the map. Still islanded by mist, we walked
into unknown land. The time was August 3rd of
1971, the day of the Agricultural Show. No self-
drive cars were available at the garage, but we
found a pleasant road to walk along. The fields
were rich with kye and crops; the cattle
intrigued me with their many colours. Barley,
bere and oats raised bedewed seed-heads to the

71

hazed sun. Turnips spread great clean blades. All the way along the verge, in the summer grass, countless spider-webs were silvered with mist-dew. By the shore of the Little Sea gold tassels of corn-thistles rose high, and on the sand grew sea-spurrey, most of its mauve, fat-seeded flowers past their best. But sea-asters still throve in perfection of setting, in clumps of lush greenery among weed and sand.

A roofless kirk came up out of the clearing mist, and we went towards it. An outside stair led up to what had once been a gallery door, but this was now iron-barred. The walls of the building were stout and strong, concrete-sealed along the top; peering through the windows, we saw strange surrealist plaster-shapes remaining upon the wall, formed by the more enduring sweeps of someone's trowel. The doors and windows had lintels of wood, no doubt cut from some of the many wrecks that in past days destroyed themselves on Sanday.

In the kirkyard were stones ancient and modern. One, near the kirk, had been erected to the memory of the captain and eight of the crew of a ship cast ashore on the island.

We followed a road between dykes and fences, passing an interesting little house that might have come out of a Disney film. It was a cottage with character; unoccupied, it gazed glassily at us from windows that wore slanting stone 'eyebrows'. All the houses had an air of endurance, standing square-shouldered to the sea-winds. Many had stepped gables. Dykes were patched with gold lichens, and bearded with grey. Old, high walls enclosed mystery; a mansion house lifted its naked chimneys to the sky. Now we could see the Show Park, where vehicles were gathered, and, at noon, we sat ourselves down on the bank of the ditch to eat. We were three, and I had prepared for two, but we seemed to have sufficient.

The Loganair plane came in, passing low over the land. We strolled up to the Show, finding the hall door still locked upon the Flower and Industrial section where judging was in progress. Further along the road we found a shop, and a very impressive church with a slender spire and ornamental windows; a building such as one might expect to see in a populous city rather than an island parish.

On returning to the Showpark we met Andrew, a kind acquaintance who took us on a tour of part of the island. We drove over a bewildering maze of roads, where I completely lost my airts, which is a common occurrence with me when away from familiar places.

We passed the new school, a spacious, many-windowed, modern structure. We saw a beautiful roadside garden made and tended by a couple in their eighties, and a hedge of varied trees planted by another lover of green things. All the gardens we saw had a profusion of flowers, and vegetables were very well advanced. Fields of crop were still pearled with moisture, but the haze was clearing and the island had wider horizons.

The old mansion house of Scar seemed mellow of stone; it was oranged over with colourful lichen. Near its enclosing dyke lay a huge granite boulder which, tradition tells, was hurled there by a witch in Shetland. It landed on the hill above, and was hauled down to Scar by fourteen horses.

"It's a meteorite, or an asteroid!" I said as we examined it. The famed Cubbie Roo of legend was in the habit of tossing great stones between

73

islands, but most of his reputed missiles are firmly planted monoliths. Perhaps this Sanday stone really did come flying through the air - though I should think that an object of that size would have buried itself if it came crashing down at meteoric speed! But, if, as reason is bound to sugest, the ice brought it, where did a glacier pick up so large a chunk of bed-rock? In Norway, say the experts.

Here we found another well-kept kirkyard to visit before taking the long road back. This is an island of long roads. In the parish of Cross and Burness we drove past Lamba Ness. Turning at an old farm road, we walked down to the cliffs. Eday had become visible, lying across the Sound; at our feet were strange, conglomerate rocks, inset with pebbles as though massive concrete works had been done there in the dawn of time. Fulmars nested on ledges in the banks, gathering themselves into spitting posture at our approach.

On our way along the road, a short time before we halted to visit the conglomerate rocks, I had observed, with a start of incredulity, a place I had 'seen' before - in a dream of a few months ago. On the way back to our host's house, he suggested that we take a walk down that very road to see the seals which were basking on a man made rock spit in the bay.

We walked down a road which was clearly familiar to me, past the houses that I had seen in my dream, towards a known shore. This kind of experience is not unique, and it is not the first dream-landscape of my life to materialise. I did not then know which part of Sanday my ancestors hailed from; my great-great-grandfather John Skea left there two centuries ago to take up residence in Shapinsay.

For all I knew, some of my kin might have lived on the shores of that bay in the past. Not to make too much of a dream - (it could scarcely be explained as race memory or reincarnation within a family because I saw the place as it is at the present day) - I suppose I became precognisant of a place I was to visit through one of these theoretical folds in time in which certain psychical researchers believe.

Somewhere upon the clifftops we found a fine fresh mushroom, which I stowed in our sandwich box to take home. Rabbits ran on the shore under the banks, nesting in caves instead of burrows. Young fulmars were fluffy and grey.

We walked over a headland and along the shore of the bay. Here were the seals, basking on the reef which the Vikings had constructed, for the bay had been an anchorage of theirs. The selkies, some grey-furred and dry, others sleekly dark with sea-water, turned their large-eyed gaze towards us. Some thought we might be dangerous, and took to the water; others lazed upon their reef and watched our approach. Round, innocent heads bobbed nearer as the men whistled and sang to them. Deserted houses were long and low by the shore. I picked up a pebble, and an ancient, battered pewter egg-cup which is now sitting on the shelf by my kitchen sink. Small ripples ran over the bay.

We crossed fields towards the road again, and walked uphill to to our friend's house where tea awaited us. Here was a greenhouse, basking in the sun, bright with flowers and rich with huge, ripening tomatoes. Geese grazed on green grass. A friendly cat came up to talk to me.

Later, before our return to the pier, we called by the Cross Kirk, beside the links. The centuries were spanned here in quietude; old, and more recent, graves shared company. The surface of the kirkyard rose and fell in heaps and hollows; I watched my feet as I trod, but no skull-deep hole opened to trap me. I wondered if this ruin might have been the kirk where the minister was reputed to have prayed, in the non-affluent days of long ago - "Oh Lord, if it be thy will to cast any puir ships ashore this day, dinna forget the island o' Sanday!"

Across the dyke, among the links, rabbits ran in colonies, and some were of an unusual shade. "There's a blue rabbit!" I said, "an' there's another. Why, the place is full o' them!" The blue-grey rabbits, we learned, were the descendants of domestic ones which had escaped and bred with their wild relatives. The half-castes were large and handsome. Even though myxomatosis has periodically cleared the ground of rabbits, the shore-dwellers have migrated in to re-colonise the area so that it does not remain rabbit-free for very long.

On our return journey the land was visible; we passed the shores of the Green Holms and the other isles. I thought of the summer lying ahead, when if the gods allowed, I might visit the North Isles again, or perhaps see the rest of Sanday.

Not for several years did I learn that my ancestors had indeed come from Pool, the locality I had recognised that day.

Two years later we again set sail, on a cool grey morning, at 6.30. Visibility was good, but for some reason I had a queasy stomach even before we left Kirkwall, probably due less to the sea than to one of these digestive upsets so common at any season. The ship went smoothly past Shapinsay, taking such a wide sweep around the Galt Skerry that I thought she was heading for Rousay. Ahead lay Eday, obscured by a rain-cloud. We passed over green and wine-dark sea. Never an easy sailor, I kept an anticipatory eye open for swells that never came. We made landfall on a fresh, rain-damp morning.

Sanday is the floweriest island it has been my good fortune to see; not only in the variety of its plants but in the variation in colourings within species. Having arrived at the Show Park, which was as yet sparsely populated, we walked on towards Cata Sand, where we took to the shore. To seaward rose high, interesting-looking dunes, appearing rather mistily through a slight shower.

"If we look carefully, we'll probably find Fyffe Robertson's footprints," I said. Prints in plenty tracked the firm sand, of birds, car tyres, and humans. Then came a kind farmer with a car, to offer us a lift across the sands to Tresness, where he was going to look at his kye. We passed over acres of hard-packed sand, an ideal place for learner-drivers. In the sunshine the dunes were blinding-bright, built of the whitest sand the world can produce, held together by limegrass, and wearing a riot of colourful plants. Here were campions of every shade between deep-rose and white; some were pale pink, some mauve, others speckled mauve-and-pink, while the albino whites had paler foliage. Sea-pinks in this area also show great variation in colour, from intense pink to white. A froth of yellow bedstraw contrasted with these, and lavender-coloured sea-rocket smelt sweet along the sands. Crystal-clear water rippled ice-green over the sand; sand built from a million-million generations of cockles, crumbled and heaped by aeons of tides.

Huge seals lay ashore at Tresness, sunning themselves on the rocks. Round, innocent heads bobbed up and down in the sea. From the other side of the bay came the sound of seal-voices, singing a song of the north wind.

Showers passed overhead, and the sun came back. Beyond the sand, after a change of vehicle, we had a swift tour of the North End, where a small community of southerners inhabit pleasant cottages. Here, too, we saw the home of a latter-day hermit, who, quite recently, had built himself a hut on the Skara Brae principle, using local materials. The round walls were made of shore stones, originally with divots between them to keep out the wind. It was roofed with bent, and its central chimney made from an oil-drum. Sandy turves had been a poor choice as draught stoppers, however, for as they dried out the sand ran away, leaving only fibre between the stones. The hermit is no longer there, but his hut remains as a curio.

A sandy sward was jewelled with wild purple pansies, very small, brilliant, and exquisite. The grass was very green, and the sea shone. White waves ran through North Ronaldsay Firth. The farm of Tafts, with its cluster of buildings, caught my eye; the roofs make a pleasing splash of deep rose, like red campion. They had all been given a coat of asbestos paint.

Arriving back at the Showpark, we studied the map, and decided to walk along a 'yellow road', past the sandy shore of Lamaness Firth.

Cattle grazed peacefully in the fields. Sanday is well-stocked with sleek handsome kye, of many breeds. When we halted in the lee of a dyke to eat a soup-and-sandwich lunch, a young gull flew down to keep us company. "Kee-yak," it said, toddling nearer, surveying us first with one eye and then the other. Given scraps of bread it snatched and swallowed them; we judged that it had been fed by visitors before. Then another whitemaa came on the scene, calling more raucously overhead, and raising the first to sit on a fence-post. Perhaps the second was warning our friend not to associate with humans, but it paid scant heed to this advice and returned to beg again.

A light shower came over Otterswick, but soon passed. Grasses blew silkenly along the verge, and corn-thistles rose on the shore, their yellow tassels just beginning to open.

We walked on, then saw on the map a place called 'mound.' Time was not in short supply, and we went down a farm road. Here we found friends and relatives of mine; I had not known of their whereabouts, and coming upon them was a very happy chance.

Here, at West Brough, we saw a unique, day-of-horse implement known as a Swedish harrow; it resembled a grubber, but had rollers with spikes on them, reminiscent of some medieval torture machine. Drawn behind a tractor, as an experiment, it had churned up the earth most efficiently, Davie told us. The mound had been a broch, and, a long time ago when the farm midden had been extended, a great deal of ash had come to light.

It was as we walked down the road towards the farm that Robin's boot-sole suddenly detached itself from its upper, much to his surprise: "I've tramped over hills in these boots for years in the stalking season," he said, "and now they have to give up - on a Sanday road!" Fortunately, our host was able to effect a good repair with copper rivets. Here we stayed for tea, rich with real cream, in a spacious and gracious house which once belonged to Walter Traill Dennison; whose name, written behind the shutter of an upstairs window, had been painted over by a previous owner of the farm.

Bidding Mary Jean and Davie farewell, we walked back towards the village in rising wind. We failed to find an acquaintance Robin had hoped to meet, but agreed that we could return again some future summer. At the hotel I brushed my wind-blown hair into something resembling order, and a chilly wind met us as we walked back towards the Cross Kirk. We strolled again through the old burial ground, and in the shelter of the dyke ate the last of our sandwiches, soup and coffee. The kirkyard enclosed graves ancient and modern, many harking back to the old days when only low memorials were allowed to lowly mortals.

Over the wall the dunes ran grey with rabbits. Not all were grey; some were blue, a breed of tame rabbits which had escaped, and several were clad in startlingly-bright ginger. The latter were the yellowest rabbits I have ever seen since the time, forty years ago, when Jim Bews and I found a nest of these in Hilton's quarry, above Ostoft's west field.

The dune grass where the Sanday rabbits ran were grey-white with eye-bright, thousand-strong to the square yard; some of the flowers were tinged with mauve, and the whole was marvellously sprinkled with pansy purple.

Sea-Road to North Ronaldsay

I woke to a shining morning, and ignoring the slight conjugal sarcasm: "You're no aye so ready tae rise!" had the entire household up in record time. Two of us had appointments in Kirkwall; Donnie with the driving tester, myself with the *Earl Thorfinn*.

"I hope it bides dry till I get me emergency stop," he remarked, surveying the sky; of this I was doubtful, as the clouds piled up and mist blew over Wideford. The rain came sudden and sharp, swimming along the decks and drenching the seats, but this was only a libation to Neptune because we sailed into clear weather.

"It'll be grand the day, so long as the wind disno rise." "We'll no hiv it this smooth all the way." "Ha-ha, thoo'll be seek afore night!" "Thir sayan we'll get a fine passage bit I hae me doots." - I heard from various quarters.

The ship slid effortlessly past Shapinsay's low banks, close to the ayre of Vasa, where the tides have carved a deep channel between the skerry and the shore. The sea ran grey, the current quiescent; dykes came down the land, bounding the green acres of Balfour Mains.

The Galt Skerry reached out to sea, and preliminary tide-rips met us; the sea danced blue, the Green Holms went past, and soon we were east of Egilsay, leaving the sunlit isle behind. But beyond us lifted the tide, and whitecaps ran up Eday's shore, where peats were still heaped on the high banks. As Rousay's craggy hills rose terraced out of the sea, I went downstairs because the lower deck did not sway so much, and gave me the illusion of swifter progress.

"We're gaun far west," I remarked to Bill Nicolson whom I found in a corner.

"Aye, it's for the tide; she's jist startan tae come in west-aboot noo. We're gaun across the tide through Westray Firth, then she'll be wi' us all the way tae North Ronaldsay."

The tide was a strong one. Great is the power that lies under that sea. I stood alone to windward, watching the great unbroken heaps of ocean come in; its foundation was unstable, and it was of great importance to me that I anticipate every lift, each watery hill that we passed over. I stood entranced but wishing not to move or speak, while we rose and fell as the tide directed. Deep indigo were the swells, the sea that had washed the coast of Labrador and had free rein across the Atlantic.

I am never seasick, being in truth a disgustingly good sailor, but a timorous one, who has only once given way to maritime nausea and then because someone was sick over my shoulder. The occasion deserves mention, it being the *Iona*'s ordeal in the teeth of a wild west gale in 1946, when the normal half-hour crossing took two hours to accomplish, and we stood off Finstown in the teeth of wind and flood until the tide turned an hour and a half later, the squat little wooden vessel dipping and heaving indomitably, and drenching her passengers forbye....

Great-hearted are the little ships. To have turned back that day would have been fatal, and why so many of us put to sea that day can only be explained by our faith in captain and ship. For years after that experience I dreaded the sea, but the dread was overcome in time; now I am only uneasy, loving the sea's motion and strength yet being disconcerted by its unpredictability.

Three birds flew by, great-winged; solans, wanderers of the ocean. At that moment, as we came into the lee of Westray, I met hamefarin' transatlantic cousins who were welcome indeed, and in the calm we went up aloft to pose for pictures. This was their first trip to North Ronaldsay and they were enjoying every moment of it.

The tidelifts were now deeply blue, shot with green and purple, and translucent overside ran strange coloured lights as the sun struck through our jumbled wake. Papa Westray faded into the northwest, Sanday came out of the sea, and North Ronaldsay drew nearer, gleaming with a beach of white sand, unique with its seawall and timeless, tiny sheep.

Stepping on to the pier I found myself alone, which is by no means unusual. I could not detect my friends in the crowd, and, as I afterwards gathered, neither could they find me.

I said "hello" to the little sheep, remarking on their slim legs and hooves like mountain goats; they are not sheep as we know them, over-fed on pasture so that they suffer from too-rapid digestion and spoiled fleeces in the spring; these deer-like sheep remind me that "the mountain sheep are sweeter but the valley sheep are fatter"; they are on a par with mountain sheep, not the fat muttons of the plain. Strange and uncan to us, they are of the old original island stock, a remnant of an Orkney that is gone.

I found myself a sandbank, with the bright sea over the wall, where fierce gales had built up the sand so that a fence surmounted the buried wall. The white sand was soft and warm, and here I sat down to write and to have a picnic.

The thistles sang with flies. Across the road to the north of the island was a lochan, and beyond the dyke sounded the ceaseless sea. Underfoot grew grass of Parnassus, eyebright in varied colours, prunella, lady's bedstraw, silverweed, forget-me-not, buttercup, dwarf mouse-ear chickweed like tiny stars, pearlwort, the round leaves of marsh pennywort and kingcup, and, rising lily-like from the water, the white-and-gold flowers of crowfoot.

A stalwart shore-stone-biggit dyke kept out the sea; finding a foothold, I saw the waves come in white-headed, while sheep watched me from the shore. Papa Westray lay almost due west; to the north, three ships converged and passed, one high and white, one belching black smoke, and all swift of way, for this is a seaway between continents.

Oystercatchers sat on the green, facing into the wind; a flock of geese grazed, enough to provide Christmas dinners for the island. A monolith, grey-bearded but less so than our Standing Stones, stood in an oatfield where the crop had the sheen of Celtic silver. Suddenly I remembered that North Ronaldsay folk grew only "black oats". But here was more bere than in the whole of the Mainland, and oh! the bloom of purple running across the cornfield under the wind! The sun beat down and the road grew long, then on the horizon I saw something I had journeyed miles to see; the Fair Isle, a blue craggy hill, and the Sheep Craig; the half-way mark to Shetland, unlike any of our island scenery.

Out of the brilliant heat came a kindly lightkeeper, to offer me a lift to the end of the road. "That's whar they pund the sheep, an' that's the dipping trough," explained the small boy who had come out for a drive with his daddy. The lighthouse, banded in white and natural brick, towered high above the sea-gusted crag, and its stair has as many steps as the 199th Psalm has verses, I was told, although I did not venture to count them. I scanned the skyline long for Foula or a tip of Shetland, but, as an islander told me later, "Foula's no up the day" - Shetland had been only briefly visible.

The Reel and Strathspey gave their afternoon concert to a packed hall. The fiddlers drew their bows in unison, and vocalists sang sweetly; Wendy Horne danced with lithe grace; a monologue provoked gusts of hearty laughter. More folk crowded in, and forms were hauled in to supplement the seating arrangements. Before the entertainment ended I sidled out of the door, because a twinge of conscience told me that my

85

presence was depriving some nice North Ronaldsay body of a seat and concerts do not cross the sea every day. The strains of Willie Grieve's fiddle followed me up the green-lined roads, and I had heard a good selection of the concert, enough to assure me of the quality of Orcadians as artistes. We take "sooth" concerts here; we ought to take Orkney concerts "sooth".

I reclined in white sand, to consume the last of my picnic, while loud squawks of anger came from a tern who was being pursued by a bonxie. Tractors and motor bikes made haste towards the pier; the piano was hoisted aboard again, and the band played "We're no awa tae bide awa", while half the island's population waved goodbye from the pier.

On the return voyage we met the sea that had thundered to the north all day; a tidal surge, the ebb in haste to leave the islands, met us at intervals all the way home. I stood by the ship's rail, gazing bemused into the depths, and wondering if, in an antique day, Homer had been a deep-sea sailor, voyaging far from home; for here was the wine-dark sea, running strongly between North Ronaldsay and Eday. Below us passed a depth of crimson, rising and effervescing into green and crystal-white; through the troubled tide shone glints of purple, indigo, mauve, rose-pink, pewter, blue, and green; all the tones detectable on a stranded jellyfish, that dying rainbow between the tides.

The Red Head of Eday appeared, illuminated in evening light, a hill cut off and dropping into the sea. Below the craig is a flat beach, unusual in such a situation in Orkney where most cliffs fall into deep water. On the slope of the headland, just before the drop, clings a wall, and as the face of the Red Head is grass-clad, this dyke must have been built to prevent sheep from slipping over; surely there can be no steeper building in Orkney than this wall attached to a slope of red clay.

Auskerry rose from the sea, a bare white tower above a mass of snowy breakers. Between the Green Holms and Egilsay we ran into a roost, which did little to slow the ship, but boiled around us with spurts of spray. To the north of Shapinsay was a choppy sea, wine-dark, froth-white, iceberg-emerald; and passing the Galt Skerry beacon we saw a bell therein, and little tystes resting on its base. Then came the quiet sea, and time to reflect on the blue bright day behind us; a memory to hold against the coming autumn rains. I came home to a dull evening, but on walking into the house found that behind my eyes was still the after-image of that shining sea, to stain the last of the day with a glowing orange-gold light.

A Visit to
Fair Isle

Years ago, when summers passed less swiftly, we had trips to the Sooth. These Highland holidays seem very far away, yet most of them took place within the last decade. We drove through rugged scenery, rock-outcropped; past, between and over hanging mountains; and occasionally, on the western skyline, we glimpsed peaked islands unlike the isles of home. More recently we explored Hoy, our western bulwark which is part of that sharp Atlantic backbone, and last summer we visited another remnant of hard, upended rock — The Fair Isle.

This was our first trip aboard the *Orcadia*. We woke to a bright morning with a hint of rain, and, arriving at the pier, watched a cosmopolitan shipload embark. Thin grey cloud impeded the sun, but as we moved out among

89

the North Isles the cloud dispersed, leaving Kirkwall, with its pale Cathedral spire, lying low in pearly haze.

The Wyre cattle float came alongside with the island contingent of trippers. Rousay folk were waiting at their pier. The tide being low, we sailed to the east of Egilsay. In the Westray Firth we felt the pull of the tide. Eday rose, dark and peat-cut, with the quarry of the Cathedral deep in its red rock, and the Red Head wearing a steep sea-wall.

Between Eday and North Ronaldsay runs a wine-dark sea. Nowhere else has our sea that colour, but here it is purple, ruby-red and indigo blue in its depths, and on its surface the waves break green. At North Ronaldsay we halted to collect more passengers, by the beach of blinding white sand. Cars and tractors were on the pier, and the distinctive accent of the islanders blended with those of Kirkwall, Rousay and USA. Outwith the dyke grazed the small, nimble sheep. The sun lay bright on sea and sand.

A long stretch of water moved between us and the Fair Isle. Among us were several 1914-18 war veteran Territorials, re-visiting one of their stations, and we were shown treasured photographs of Fair Isle folk at their daily work a half-century ago. Wind and tide were against us, but presently Foula came up, a blue horizon-bubble, and the Fair Isle stood ahead, unreal in the waste of ocean; high, craggy, and looking as though determined to remain there in spite of wind and water. The tip of Shetland lay beyond, sunlit and nearer than Orkney.

To me the Fair Isle has a mirage quality. Solid, and tilted towards the south, where still it rises on tall cliffs, that green, white-lighthoused eminence is scarcely credible. To add to the sense of illusion the Sheep Craig is like a miniature Rock of Gibraltar; a lion couchant, patient against savage seas. Rocks drive their teeth into the bed of the ocean to hold the island there, and lift it out of the waves' reach.

Houses clustered under brown hills and the snowy lighthouses gleamed. Rock falls were jagged below the cliffs, but the perpendicular rock strata was quite unlike that of our under-cut western seaboard.

Arctic skuas skimmed the ship, and bonxies were over the hills. The *Good Shepherd* ferried us ashore at the North Haven, where we obtained transport to the more populous south end of the island, where most of the company went to have tea in the hall.

Stepping over a fence, we took to the open country. Black, deep-bodied cattle grazed, tethered by field-sweeping ropes, three times the length of any tether I had previously encountered. They were bonny kye, sleek and heavy. To the north a gloup opened, slanting down to a shingle beach.

Among the sparse heather and prostate juniper grew ground-level jasione montana, blue buttons on harsh green and brown velvet; the heather was not yet in bloom. A singularly deep-pink variety of ragged robin, short-stemmed but large-flowered, flourished by the edge of the pasture land.

We spread the map on the hillside, and the island sprang to life, with every rock, field, geo, burn and knowe named. Time forbade the exploration of the entire island, but our path took us along the heights where we had a clear view. The hills and coastline of Shetland intrigued us. There rose Sumburgh Head, with tall masts, and Fitful Head, we thought; but

91

other pale shores, lifted by refraction, remained unidentified. Foula, and the Knowe of Foula, stood far out to sea.

In a peat-black pool I found a much-dwarfed variety of spearwort, and an ivy-leaved water-crowfoot. Two small whirlwinds passed us, swishing coldly through the summer day, lifting loose vegetation and feathers, and swirling away with a noise like distant aircraft. In such a situation they could well have been the slip-stream of something alien to our world; but never a space-craft darkened the day, and presently a pair of everyday planes brought back reality, one proceeding sedately south from Shetland, the other swifter and higher, preceding its thunder-clap of sound.

We walked downhill, climbing a stout dyke that divided the fields. This wall resembled the Stromness dykes, but was built of sparkling pink sandstone instead of granite. Venerable lichen clung to it, as long and grey-green as that on our Standing Stones.

On level land was the emergency airstrip, but the hill belonged to the skuas. They resented us and said so, mewing overhead, swooping with windy wings, and adapting the time-honoured technique of the 'broken wing', while the young birds watched, unaware of the reason for their elders' agitation.

Near the sheltered shore the jasione grew taller, and its sky-blue flowers ornamented the cliffs where puffins eyed us with unconcern. Under heathery banks, in soft, black peat-stoor, sheep had sheltered as they do in the Highlands. The peat, instead of being firm and deep, seemed very crumbly compared to that at home.

Sumburgh Roost had risen before we left the hilltop; as we walked towards the pier we saw the swell curl around the foot of the craigs, and break on the inshore rocks.

At anchor, the ship rose and fell gently; the seas were long and slow. Our exodus was protracted, because now the *Good Shepherd* lifted to the swells, and boarding the *Orcadia* was more difficult than leaving her.

Everyone had acquired a tan, and a thirst possessed us. Tango and coffee went down with the sandwiches left aboard the ship. The last of the passengers leapt aboard, and we sailed out into the gently heaving sea, rounding the north of the island this time. Here the hills fall steeply into deep water, great chasms open, and rock teeth upthrust. Those legendary Armada survivors must have had the good fortune to be wrecked near one of the few accessible beaches, for to land below the craigs that almost entirely surround the island would have meant certain destruction.

North Ronaldsay was long in coming; the sun was still with us, but as we passed between the isles darkness came, lit in the north by a band of rose-red blending into gold, above a blue that was inseparable from green. We left our Rousay shipmates and went home over shining black-green water, patterned by tide-ripples and pools of calm. A red moon came up over the land, an unearthly thing afire; and half the folk of Kirkwall stood aboard the pier as it sailed serenely to meet us, trailing midnight-blue water with golden shafts of light.

Birsay's
Northern Shore

A good few weeks ago there shone a sunny
Sunday. We went west-about, past fields of pale
grain, and pastures of full-grown lambs, taking
the road leading to the North Side of Birsay. The
Brough reached out to sea, and Kitchener's
Memorial rose to the west. Southward hung a
haze in the sky but the day was mild.

A field's breadth from these ocean-worn
crags stands a string of houses, a stronghold of
the old Orkney, a district where the Vikings
lodged. This village opened the first window in
Birsay, boldly letting in a small light in the days
of the window-tax, and the frail square of
lamp-light issuing thence on a night of storm
saved a grateful ship from the rocks as she drove
around Marwick Head.

Here, too, when the new road was laid down,
came into view an earthen floor a spade's depth

below the surface; a blue-clay, solid-packed floor as hard as stone, with a square, burnt flagstone hearth in the centre. Today the houses stand resolutely in grey stone, weathering the storms that sweep up over the fields, sheltering folk whose ancestors took much of their living from the sea.

Our host, a Birsay man with four centuries of local tradition in his blood, led us towards the shore. Up this road has come many a cubbie of fish, and in his childhood, he told us, early mornings sounded with hard leather seaboots 'tonkan' along the metalled surface at four o'clock.

Skippi Geo has been a boat noust since Viking days. Here the longships were hauled; here more modern fishermen winch up their boats to safety in the hollowed green. This is a long geo with grassy banks; at its northern end is a headland landmarked by a whalebone. In the geo is a Boat Well; now drying up, I am tempted to think, from lack of use.

Dry seapinks shone papery-pale, a low smoke of spray misted under Marwick Head; the sea was polished by sun and offshore breeze. Every rock along the coast is named; below us rose two large rock-formations, the Inner Castle and Outer Castle, separated from the crag by a trink of sea where cuithes may be fished from the rocks; our Birsay man has seen silver herring fry in there, pursued by feeding cuithes. Among names of Norse extraction here is an alien: Donkey's Hole; did a memorable donkey fall in, or come ashore? A rock, black and twisted by volcanic action, is Skirr Brett, and along here is the Pow o' Stighton.

The shore is changing, for we came to recent rockfalls as we followed the path, once deeply worn through the bare earth but now only trodden into the overgrowing turf. An intrusive iron dyke cuts through the rock strata, and at the beginning of this dyke is a pool recommended for bathing, where tide-water gathers among sun-warmed rocks.

We paused by the upstanding weathered bone of the ninety-foot whale which once came ashore in Doonagooa. By the point of Netherqueena is the rock Sowaskirr; here the rock strata have been folded as if a book had been bent into a right angle. The Noup Head Light shone whiter than foam, elevated on pale purple hills, sixteen miles across the sea from the Lighthouse on the Brough.

This dip, with a rock at each side, is a saw-pit where of old sea-borne logs were sawn up while suspended between the stones, and here is the Round Geo, sea-hollowed out of mellow clay. In the short turf is a boulder, one of the 'Mansie's' stones that reputedly mark the resting place of St Magnus' body on its progress from its landing at the Evie shore to its ultimate rest in Kirkwall.

The sea swirled around the Shippy Rock, Rearnaskirr and Slidy Back, that reaching sea, now quiescent, that has broken so many unwary vessels on the angry rocks. On the cliff-top is the grave of one Captain Wright, flung ashore in a wild winter sea and buried with a gold ring on his finger; the only survivor of that wreck was a Tammie Cowie, who was found sitting dazed in a byre in the early morning with no idea as to how he had struggled out of the sea, over the rocks, across the field and through the first available door to safety. That wreck brought relief to the folk dwelling near, because after a hard year fuel was scarce: the poor ship that the 97

Good Lord had seen fit to cast upon their shore had been laden with tar, which kept the fires burning for the rest of the winter.

We passed Siller-a-geo, and another Mansie's Stane. (Were the bearers weary along this gusted coast; did the sea blow cold upon them, so that they laid down their burden to beat warmth into their hands?) Here, too, lay a more recent block of stone, weighing perhaps three-quarters of a hundred-weight, which a high sea picked up and tossed like a pebble; the same sea which dislodged from the cliff-edge a small earth pinnacle and deposited it intact some distance inland where it still lies. The ironstone intrusion appeared again, a barrier against the sea, and inside grew sea campion. On the clifftop flourished a dense plantation of cast-out garden marguerites, slightly smaller than their cultivated originals but thriving. I remember walking along this shore, perhaps a decade ago, and noting a glorious profusion of matricaria maritima such as I have never seen since, for each flower was double, the yellow centres being obscured by a mass of white petals. To my discredit be it said - I did not collect a single specimen to substantiate the discovery.

Here is a well which fills slowly, whence long ago folk carried their water; and it was not unknown for the weary goodwife to fall asleep while the slow spring dripped, so that another could step in out of turn and steal the water! This is Hesta Geo; that rock is Polabar.

A rock rises like a wall and the sea is deep inshore where the *Keith Hall* was wrecked. This was originally a German trawler vintage 1914; her plates were still inscribed in German.The waves threw her close inshore, and in the face of that rock is a peg driven for the use of the small boat which came in from the rescue tug.

Caves were underfoot; we trod hollow ground. Seaward was the rock castle of Boondas; there was Tama Grana. Limpet shells were white and scattered on a pinnacle where oystercatchers had nested and fed. The engines of a wreck rose barnacled nearby.

In the face of the shore is a quarry once used for housebuilding, square-cut from geometric slabs. A hare sat, ears high, just over the fence, then vanished with apprehensive leaps along the shore.

This shore gave precarious coverage to those who would escape the Press Gang. A sudden narrow cleft in the rock leads, to all appearances, straight down to the cold green sea; but closer inspection reveals a square hole under the upper rockslab, just large enough to accommodate one with a steady head who had good reason to hide. This hidey-hole, or the rock, is Braga.

Past here, through a turbulent sea, the North Side folk once watched a trawler lurch in distress to founder in Eynhallow Sound, and after her went the old Stromness Lifeboat seeming in imminent peril herself, disappearing intermittently between freezing winter waves.

Fantastic cliff scenery lies washed bare; the rocks of Sanshween with zig-zag folded strata. Skerries lie flat in Cliv Geo; inshore are dulse rocks where people once gathered seafood. This is a good fishing geo. Inside the fence we again walked on hollow ground; out there we saw the Point of Whitaloo, and Glebeness Skerry, a square tablet dropping into deep water.

When we arrived at Longaglebe skarfs sat as

99

always on the base of the farther craigs, and fulmars whitened the ledges where the 'grip' pours water collected out of Birsay Hill. This is probably the longest geo in Orkney, terminating in a small cave; the water is deep, and a boat may come in with safety only if no white sea breaks over the rocks at the entrance. Once, our Birsay friend told us, he had rowed into the geo when a white wave broke with a surge behind. This meant that the swell was about to rise, and by the time the fishermen emerged into the land-sea their boat was bobbing crazily between the crests.

"Boy, I wir sayan me prayers," he told us. "I wir never so small in me life. It's strange hoo peedie you feel in such a moment o' crisis, matchan your insignificance against the awful pooer o' the sea!"

Switha with
Seals and Terns

Sunday began cool and grey, streaked with mares' tail above cumulus. We took the Old Road to Kirkwall, passing more road-works where a corner is being stream-lined, and fields of sheep with swathes cut through their pasture so that they have a 'face' from which to begin grazing. Wild pansies raised kitten-like faces; a ginger tom hunted the verge. Foxgloves and willowherb had swamped the hedge of whin so richly golden earlier in the year. Under a lowering sky, dark streaks ran across the sea. We were half-way to Kirkwall when we had to reverse our tracks, after suddenly discovering that we had left home penniless. Disconsolate lapwings sat in the ebb as we returned by the shore road; the sky had been swept clean to leave a blue day. A fisherman cycled out of Kirkwall wearing ten-gallon boots. A boat, coming through the String, flung out white bow-waves.

Our Field Club rendezvous was by the Power Station, and there we halted in the sun. A white butterfly glimmered out of an open door.

We travelled the road that holds apart the seas, and to the west were whitecaps while westwards sparkled a sheet of living silver. Bathers dipped in the sandy bay.

South Ronaldsay was dotted with hay-coles, and the wind ran across fields of golden-green and blue-green oats. A tanker, small with distance, passed through the sea-lane. From Sandwick we embarked for Switha, to my considerable unease because the wind was freshening and we were voyaging near the Pentland.

Puffins and tystes paddled out our way, and jellyfish abounded. This is their season, when every tide runs full of pulsing life, in orange and sea-weed brown, purple and lavender, cold blue, and translucent pearl-grey with four-leaved clover design. They floated resistlessly, going with the current, expanding and contracting, trailing their streamers.

We landed on red-ware at Switha, to be met by flocks of frantic terns. A sea-urchin and starfish crept on the rock where I stepped ashore. Seals gathered to survey us, and all along the east shore their curious round heads surfaced; one, in a geo, we saw as a luminous green body where it trod water, its back shining like sand.

On this shore the rocks were horizontal, and we stepped down terraces where fulmars nested. Many gulls were here, young and speck-led, with stubby tails and patches of down still among their feathers. They sat tight-packed in any available hollow, appearing suddenly underfoot. Surprisingly few fledglings were to be seen all over the island; this is not a good bird year. Little fluffy fulmars, deceptively like adorable toys, rose in their ledge-nests to threaten us with streams of oil. From a geo several shags flew out, clad in rich green.

White waves were in the Firth; Swona lay to the south-east, and the cool breeze came inshore from the North Sea. Gulls, overhead, seemed to laugh maliciously at my anxious seaward glances. Brown weedlaces streaked the rocks below; a puffin sat on the edge of the crag, absurd of beak and wearing a black collar. Sea-spleenwort crept along clefts, green and shiny, and stagnant opaque pools lay above the tide's reach, that tide now running quietly in deep lily-pad swirls, grey as molten metal under the passing clouds. A odour of guano came up the cliffs; on ledges below were the gulls' dining-tables, littered with a multitude of limpet shells.

Our party had become divided. Deer-like, on the skyline, stood flocks of watchful sheep. The army has been on Switha, for concrete foundations remain here and there, and traces of much earlier occupation can be seen in the bronze-age burials, each mound having been hacked into by the treasure-seeking Vikings who plundered every grave of its goods, even in outlying isles.

On the south-west tip of the island I found a knowe with stones on edge, and right on the cliff edge was a mysterious circle of stones like a steethe, though whether or not this is of antique construction remains a matter for conjecture.

Cantick Head was directly in front of us, in 103

the sun's path, the lighthouse snow-white beyond the tide race of liquid silver. A reef jutted out into the turmoil of seas that ran both ways with wind and tide. Longhope sheltered the village, and the elongated range of Hoy sloped upwards to the north.

Rock pipits were loud among the shore downy-grey of plumage. A pipit exploded from my feet, leaving a dainty nest of dark-fleeced, yellow gaping babies.

Botanically Switha is not exciting, and even the bogs were waterless; there seemed to be no fresh water on the island, no springs or pools. One of the Standing Stones marked on the map is venerably bearded with lichen.

Geologically there is more of interest because the eastern extremity would appear to be hollow, with a miniature gloup and a strange depression termination in one of those unfathomed depths, mossy-sided and fern-grown. Seen from the sea the cliffs are pillared, and long caves probably penetrate well inland. We went home over a sea which everyone assured me was ideal; the boat rose and fell on the swells with buoyancy, but I am am apprehensive sailor and South Ronaldsay's crags were welcome. These, spectacularly cut into pillars, we saw to advantage with the evening sun; long red clay banks, and a backward-sloping headland with natural arches, we passed on our way back to Sandwick. In thatsuntrap bracken and bushes grew in purple flower, and honeysuckle was sweet on the incoming breeze. Still the jellyfish came with us, helpless voyagers of the ocean currents. In the gathering cool of the evening we saw the boat come up to her slipway, then, past fields of contented kye, we took the long road home.

The Colours of our Landscape

*E*arlier in the season our landscape lies in muted shades, so delicate that to the jaded eye they appear indescribably drab. Now, although our home-stretch of moorland offers mainly the 'natural' tones used in 'Fair Isle' patterns, I need not go far afield to find colours to delight the eye, for gold and white are gleaming, along with variety of tender greens and a glory of blue.

Not long ago I witnessed the shimmer of blue and pink along our coastlines, cast by a multitude of sea-pinks and scillas. Grasses in bloom have colours that change with the wind; across hayfields move waves of wine-red, plum-purple, haze-blue, deep green, and, with a rising breeze, living silver.

Just to look at the cultivated fields and the marsh sends a shiver of delight through the soul. Who can resist those buttercup pastures, 105 those lemon-yellow acres of sweet-smelling runcho, hedges of wild parsley, blowing down of white-silver cotton, crimson-dotted bogs and mauve-speckled moors? When I see a sheen of ragged robin, or a riot of rosy campion, I am apt to go into a dwam. That is why we are at a standstill. Something catches my eye, and like the poet Davis I must stand and stare. What is this life anyway? We must enjoy these aesthetic pleasures; they may not come our way again.

Wild pansies are blue in the headrigs, but the bluest thing I ever seen opened on a headland. It is only lately that I have come to appreciate blue flowers, but how wonderful they are upon a grey day. Meadow–cranesbill, which runs riot in a garden, enhances the natural vegetation of verges where the overspill has been planted, and I remember a tourist who halted a bus long enough to pick himself a specimen.

On a sunless day I saw a blue shore. The sands were golden, not the burnished yellow of kingcups but a subdued true gold; overhead cried terns, and one fluffy baby ran frantically among the stones.

Rounding the corner we saw it - a shelf of blue, as if a lake of deep water stretched between the dunes, binding the dry sand, grew massed hillocks of mertensia maritima, or oyster-plant, each neat round meeting the next so that they formed a solid front of blue. The large rosettes of blue-green leaves trailed flower-stems evenly down from the centre; the sky-blue flowers opened more profusely on the seaward side.

Six of us went to Egilsay on a close grey day. Mist shrouded Hoy and the Mainland hills, and a small rain, something less than dew, merely touched us in passing. Along the Rendall road sacks of peat awaited carting, reminding me that I was playing truant. Sheets of ragged robin and bog cotton shimmered over the land.

We arrived early at Tingwall; across the sea came the sound of a boat's engine, but the source was hidden in the soft haze. Fulmars sat tamely on low cliff ledges, looking gentle and soft of plumage, but making ominous noises at our approach, obviously with a view to sending us away smelling vilely. Their white throats seemed to pulse with gathering oil, and we speculated on the range and accuracy of their spit. An iron-stone 'dyke' ran in from the sea.

White, and effortless as a fulmar, our transport came in to the pier; a hidden bright-ness filled the air as we moved past skerries and the low shore of Wyre. Terns flew overhead carrying small fish. Rousay's fields were colour-ful but mist trailed from the hills.

Between us and Egilsay a turmoil became resolved into a school of porpoises. Sleek backs and curved dorsal fins rose and fell; we caught up with them but they suddenly submerged to reappear some distance astern, still leaping and plunging, full of the joy of life.

On Egilsay our party became divided, we three botanists scrambling through fences in search of bog plants and getting left behind. This is the orchid season, and some of these were asking to be photographed.

One entrancing morass made gulping noises as we waded through it, occasionally an unwary foot sank down into thick black odorous ooze. Despite a suspicion that this might be a man-eating bog which tempts its prey with flowers, we navigated it in safety. I only once got caught on barbed wire, but I lost a button - a silly button which fitted together like a snap fastener. Now

107

I have only the centre part; the remainder is at the bottom of a ditch below St Magnus Kirk.

This landmark, so impressive with its tall tower, is built, in a fashion reminiscent of Noltland Castle, with great blocks of stone enhancing the design of the masonry. A flutter of wings made me duck back out of the tower as a pigeon took its departure.

A loch lay by the east shore, full of pond-weeds, persicaria in bloom and bogbean; a lovely place in which to fish for plants, although we were later informed that such wading was dangerous. Many seals swam offshore, and one, lying on a rock and idly flapping its tail, was a pale creamy colour, but when viewed through a glass proved to be dry and fluffy instead of sleek and dark.

Elders swam in flocks, with strings of little ones bobbing like creel corks, the mothers crooning with a deep guttural note, answered by the higher-pitched voices of the babies. A handsome sheldrake stood preening his feathers. Three friendly farm dogs did not bark at our intrusion; in fact none of our company encountered a single noisy dog, although the same cannot be said for the oyster-catchers who cried resoundingly as though we were trespassing.

On a tractor-trailer a graceful boat came down to take the sea at Sand Geo. Investigating a rocky brae we aroused the interest of a red-polled bull, who ambled across the field, bogling all the way. He did not wish us any harm for he looked benevolent rather than aggressive, but we could still hear him lifing up his voice when a whole wide valley lay between us.

From the hilltop we saw a strong tide race through Howie Sound, carrying ducks swiftly past and giving added momentum to the lovely boat we had seen earlier. Two eiders, trying to swim eastwards, made heavy weather of the current. Rousay had come out of the haze and Kierfea hung reflected darkly on the tide-swirled glassy sea.

Geologically this island has almost a West Highland aspect in its outcrop of rock, sudden lochans and marshes. At the northern end the strata are vertical. Here has been tumultuous upheaval in the deep when continents and islands were being shaped.

On the homeward voyage we ate a belated tea, for two of us had left our provisions in the care of our menfolk. Coffee, still at boiling point, splashed from my defective Thermos which one of these days will be the victim of a deliberate accident.

Shoals of jellyfish pulsated in with the tide, and we passed over submerged reefs where sand shone green beside redware. Our wake had a bloom like velvet, a jumbled crystal velvet with a violet glow of jade and turquoise. All around lay Elysian isles on a milk-white sea, and a whiter boat, returning, greeted us again in passing. Upon such stormless seas comes a detached, mental tranquillity, a slowing-down of tempo in which the world runs smoothly, a buoyancy of spirit seldom experienced on land.

Shapinsay Revisited

A cool grey evening followed a breezy Saturday afternoon. There was a late boat to Shapinsay; I phoned a warning of our impending arrival in the middle of the night.

A shower reached Kirkwall with us, streaming straight down my neck as I opened the car door. Aboard the *Orana* we proceeded smoothly across the String.

We trod a road we have walked before, many a time in the days that are gone. Past the silent sleeping village, around the Bay of Elwick and up the brae where the phone wires sing no more; past the Memorial which was our twice-weekly rendezvous in 1940 when all the land lay lightless, tight and vulnerable in the grip of war; by the hedge where sparrows rustled, along the familiar stretch between Hilton's fields and down the farm road home, where cattle sighed gently in their sleep, the burn bubbled under the brig, the trees breathed a welcome and the sea sang.

Morning came in with a hint of rain and a fresh breeze. We walked 'ower the Brae' to unlock the Kirk door and set things to rights before the service. From the gallery window I saw a thin grey shower cloud the Firth hills and come mistily over the sea. The clock had to be set to the correct time, that patient old-timer which has ticked the services away for over a century, and which, by an over-zealous winding, I once caused to strike during Communion. Many years ago, with much care and not a little importance, I helped carry it to be repaired by a canny clock-member now in the kirkyard.

A swap-wind streaked around the corner of the Kirk. Clouds, hard and oily-dark like shale, built up to let sharp showers fall. In the roofless chapel which is the burial place of the Balfours a bush of white veronica grows. This has seeded itself with marvellous abandon, so that brave small seedlings, hanging on like stonecrop, are rooted in crevices of the wall, living on 400-year-old lime. Escallonia, neatly trained along the eastern wall of the Kirkyard, is bright with polished leaves, and ivy clings to the church wall; but the cotoneaster that grew below window-level, winter-crimson in my memory, is gone, and a once familiar variegated elder has also vanished.

Old kirkyards are fascinating. In a new cemetery we keep respectfully to the path, but the occupants of older acres have been there so long that they do not mind our treading on their grass.

Here, in the lower corner of the burial ground, lie a family wiped out by a deadly 'black' fever in 1882. In the shadow of the church, where the windowless north wall used to give me a certain feeling of awe, lie the victims of a boating tragedy; five people who were drowned while crossing from Carness on their way to Communion in Shapinsay.

Sandstone and granite slabs grow lichen, black marble stands tall, white marble scrolls tell of bairns laid to their last sleep, and recumbent weathered stones have endured long. Foot-high slabs are a reminder of the bad old days when landlords decreed that their tenants must be lowly even in monument. A marble plaque on the outside of the Lairds' tomb bears a verse by David Balfour in honour of a faithful friend and servant. But the 1951 hurricane gave many of the stones a lean, and further gales have rocked and loosened them in their foundations so that they stand at varying angles; and here we have a problem facing most communities: who is to take care of these tombstones and set them straight, when the relatives of the deceased are gone?

We went over the dyke and down to the shore, where the wind met us with a bluster of rain. Part of Steiro has fallen in, leaving the building on the outer wall of the broch exposed. Green weed clad the sandstone slabs where ripple-marks of an ancient shore have been petrified; the free-quarry stagnated in its algae-green water, below the face where seapinks cling. Tall, golden-rayed corn thistles were ranged along the banks and orache rose in a wave on the pebbled foreshore, nurtured on black-dried ware.

Later, as waves ran past the noust, we wandered westward. Blue shreds of sky ran between cloud-banks. Here lay a long-travelled rubber-boot, wearing barnacles and tufts of 113 weed. Plastic ferns sprang among the stones, with a foam of matricaria spraying out to either side. Kye-trodden primroses scattered the hollow of the second noust, first-year plants intent on being ready for spring. Around the corner scillas were in seed, and tiny, deep-purple eyebright rose in pockets of salted earth. Four dark dunters and a large seal eyed us uncertainly; we were occupying their landing place.

The branstickle pow, long, green and spring-fed, lay as of old in an angle of the slanting rocks. Inganess Geo, with its fishing rock which became a fortress for our bairns, has not changed; the ripples chased me over the shingle, red anemone blobs subsided into crevices above the tide and opened flowery tentacles below. Sea-milkwort outlined the seams of stone.

We halted in the Well Geos, where segs raised tall swords beside a brackish spring. Stranded jellyfish, lavender coloured with a four-leaved clover design, seemed made of more solid material than the large, melting brown and purple gelatinous bodies that come in helpless drifts in autumn to die among the rocks. The shore slopes steeply below the Fort and along Liviness Geo; the contorted strata match those at the Head of Work, where the same upheaval has disgorged them.

In the geo floated long hair-like tresses of brown weed, streaking out across the sand. Terns flew overhead as we neared the reef of Hellyar Holm. The heavy steel target at the old firing range, used by the Volunteers, the Territorials, and the Rifle Club in their turn, bore marks of heavier Army fire that had bitten into its surface.

Elwickbank pier, now in disuse, is falling down. A small avalanche of stones had slipped into the ebb since our last visit. Varied jetstem strewed the bay, tide-borne.

Rubbish is becoming more permanent year by year. Tins will eventually rust away, glass will break and wear into jewels among the pebbles, but plastic articles bid fair to last for ever. Such things as liquid-soap containers should not be put into rubbish-tips; they will burn, if care is taken to cut them open to prevent their bursting in the fire.

We walked up the Back Road beside the plantation, past the Castle tennis court (where of old I tried to play tennis but frequently failed to hit the ball), and under a canopy of branches towards Sound. The trees had an uneasy motion and their leaves 'hirseled' as an oatfield does in autumn. Closing the gate behind us, we turned towards the shore. A golden glory of stonecrop clad the walls and dykes of Sound. The plantation turns its back to the west, behind its sheltering wall; the trees rise in height from the level of their shelter, each row overtopping the one behind in a wind-ordered slope.

It was an evening of strange dark light, of lucidity rather than light, cold with indigo cloudbanks over which raced drifts of smoke-grey. Sheep moved in the field, under command of the shepherd and his dog, in a fluid woolly entity. The sea washed a low shore; here was the remains of a lime kiln and below it, spilling into the ebb, a vein of calcite. Broken pieces of this held imprisoned pebbles, and in one we found a shell, stained grey; an oyster, aeons old. The castle faced the shore, beyond soft undulations of green turf.

The wind followed us up Elwick Bay, where many of the hawthorns in the hedge are dying, 115 age-brittle and lichen-grey. The moon, just-by the full, came up redly with a harvest face, and the sober Aberdeen-Angus cattle in the field pranced, skipped like lambs and snorted like bulls as we walked down the road, evidently excited by the weather change manifest in the wild sky.

On Monday we sailed steadily back across the String in the face of a strengthening wind, and my pockets bulged with the spoils of our walk: a mussel shell, lipped with mother o' pearl, measuring rather more than five inches in length; a piece of another mussel, inside which had grown a pair of large barnacles like snowy volcanoes; a fragment of calcite; that fossilised shell; and a rattling colony of flat winkles in orange, olive, brown, gold and grey, whorled and wonderfully made.

The Purple Tracts
of Eday

We found a bright and breezy day in Eday, after leaving the Mainland clouded and grey. As Shapinsay went astern of the *Orana* and Wideford Hill grew smaller, a widening line of blue opened before us and a sun-shot sea leapt out of the north-east. The boat, swung by the choppy waves coming through Spurness Sound, lurched against the pier as we climbed the ladder, and Eday, long and dark lay before us.

This is an island where depopulation shows. There is a new school, generously windowed, for a declining number of bairns. Acre upon acre of hill lies unclaimed. The roads are good, but the ways are lonely. We had time to visit one side of the island only, taking the road that led to Carrick. Seen from the North Isles boat, the west side appears more populous.

We passed the kirk where a service was in progress, the War Memorial standing high, and two empty churches. By the roadside grew massed purple heather bells, more brilliant than any I have ever seen elsewhere, and sheets of a very lovely grass which I remember of old. Its name I have forgotten for the moment; we called it everlasting grass, and picked bouquets of it to adorn the ben mantlepiece. In Shapinsay it was less common, growing in bunches here and there along road verges, but in Eday we found it in quantity, blowing silkily purple, silver and green, for an albino strain added variety to the original.

It is several weeks since we visited Eday, and now, wherever I go, I see tracts of this grass shining in waste places and along verges. The prevailing weather conditions of each particular year gives prominence to certain plants; this year we have a superabundance of bog cotton, this handsome grass, hogweed, and angelica.

Tall foxgloves grew in Carrick Wood, purple and white. Brown and golden velvet bees crept in and out of the flowers. Here I found myself enclosed by trees; gnarled limbs reached out for me, dripping with lichen. A wren called loudly as I waded through thick vegetation that concealed drainage trenches and hollows.

A dark, muddy-bottomed lochan was querulous with skuas. Swift pirates swooped on indignant terns. Close inshore, through a haven of rushy channels crept a teal and her tiny brood, miraculously hidden from the skuas.

The Calf of Eday sheltered the Sound. A fishing boat lay at anchor. On the beach I collected several pebbles, and two beautiful stones to weigh down my haversack. One was of red granite, alien to this shore, and the other glittered in silver-grey and pink: granite with an inset of mica. Did the Ice Age bring them here, or have they come as ballast? I walked, heavily laden, up the hill, meeting a tiny rabbit in the sheep-enclosure.

Swept by generations of northeasters, the plantation on Vinquoy Hill is deceptive. Seen from the outside it is a strange low maze of large trunks with thin and crooked branches, but there are taller trees within. On that steep hillside setting it wears a primeval aspect, as though it were no recent thing but a survival from our peat-bank forests. The wind cried higher up the hill with a foreboding voice, and long lichens clad the tortured trees. I dared not enter this fey place lest I never be seen again.

Entrancing things were at my feet; our tiniest flowering plant, the minutely branching all-seed, radiola linoides; and eyebright, in a bewildering range of colours, shapes and sizes. While I lagged behind, collecting specimens, my man struck across the moor towards a burial mound; I found him sitting on the remains of a stalled cairn.

The most impressive stone I have yet seen standing rises on this moor, looking like a gigantic upraised hand. A sandstone monolith, it has split, weirdly, into three fingers green-lichen-grown above and cattle-rubbed below.

Red-throated divers rose from Mill Loch. By the Baptist Kirk gentians opened, darkly blue. Eday is almost cut in two between the Bay of London and the Loch of Doomey. We followed the abandoned road across the sands; fine red-green sand, almost like that of Rackwick, sank beneath our feet, but did not sing as we passed. Walking back, we had time to admire the royally-coloured heather bells that rang along

119

the fences. The hills were still sombre, but what a transformation must come over that island in the autumn! Black, rich peat was stacked beside the road. The scent of heather bloom, and of peat fires, moved on the air.

Homeward bound, in Stronsay Firth, we examined our botanical booty. For my own pleasure I carried home several large, deep-crimson curly-doddies gathered along the road to the pier, and one in a peculiar shade that could only be described as blue. A blue clover must be a freak; I have seen roses in a similar cold, unlikely colour, which was rare and unusual several years ago.

Our boatman took us home past the East Craigs of Shapinsay, a wild and pillared shore. Great caves open, in which sizeable boats could hide; one such opening is reputed to reach far inland, and, seen from the sea, the tradition seems credible. From the Fit o' Shapinsay the shore slopes down to the Cumlins o' Maovi, then to quiet green banks. Through binoculars we picked out the farms, in snow-white and grey, lying to the sun.

The String was quiet as we passed the slanting cliffs and the lighthouse of Hellyar Holm, but we swung on the tide near Thieves' Holm. The brightness of the sea still shone behind my eyes as evening darkened down.

The High
Road of Rousay

*T*he morning was grey and raw, but while I got breakfast visibility improved; I could now see the Stromness road.

"We're in for a day o' rain," declared my man as he surfaced.

"That's a sure sign o' a bonny day," I answered. A subdued brightness hung on the horizon as we left home, but swirls of grey met us in Rendall and Rousay was scarcely visible from Evie Pier. In view of the heavily bedewed grass I was wearing rubber boots; before the day was out I could cheerfully have thrown them over the craig.

Our party divided on arrival at Rousay, the larger number setting out to ring fulmars. Five of us obtained transport to Scockness, driving along a once-familiar road, past the mill and the Sourin burn; there we saw that the New Zealand

121

flax wore great spikes of dark red bloom. There was a boat in the Bay of Ham and another beached on the quiet shore.

We visited the kirkyard, climbing over a stile. This burial ground has been designed to circumvent the Devil, having no conventional entrance where he could get in, only a series of steps with a gate on top which has to be lifted off. No trace remains of the chapel which once kept guard.

A vague island appeared to the east as we walked towards the Loch of Scockness. Rocky outcrops, similar to those in Egilsay, were underfoot. Here we found a gull which had died in peculiar circumstances. Its legs were bound tightly together with a piece of string which had cut into them, immobilising its feet and causing a slow and painful death. Had it become entangled with this string at sea and been unable to free itself? Surely no person would perpetrate such an atrocity.

A red buoy sailed on the loch, and pond-weeds lifted their heads. Here I found a patch of hedge woundwort, the rarer parent of our common and rather handsome hybrid. The flowers are of a darker hue than those of the hybrid and more frowningly hooded; the leaves more heartshaped and with a longer stem. (The other parent plant, marsh woundwort, is narrower of leaf and flower-cluster, and the leaves are stemless.)

Islands came and went as we rounded the shore, then stabilised themselves as the rising breeze blew shreds of sky into sight. This is a sea-gusted coast, but the close turf wore jewels; Grass of Parnassus less than an inch in height, its white cups lying flat on the green; orchids, late of arrival, appearing straight out of the earth; prunella, rich purple and orchid-sized;

tiny pink geraniums, forget-me-not; kidney vetch; and little creeping ferns, all with no stems to speak of. Scilla pods split to reveal black seeds, and primrose leaves lay flat. Every tiny hollow was gossamer-webbed and dewed.

The terraced Head of Faraclett seemed as steep as Hoy. While we toiled upwards, sheep bounded merrily along the skyline and a little black rabbit bobbed away. The rock strata lay flat, except for a few iceborne boulders which stood on edge. From the hilltop we saw Westray come up clearly, with Fittie Hill wearing a cloud, and the Noup Head Lighthouse gleaming whitely out to sea. A sparkle ran over the blue water below, but the hillside fell alarmingly into it, giving the impression that one false step would cause a Gadarene rush towards destruction. Under the cliffs the sea was deeply blue and shadowed, for the hill hid the sun.

In the valley grey stone houses sheltered, some of them empty, but seeming as if they had grown there, being built of the native stone. Tiny silvery willows crept on the terraces, some berried with galls, each holding a grub. We scrambled over two substantial dykes and took a sheep-track along an abominable slope, even more awesome than the side of Hoy's Ward Hill because of the sea below. Kierfea rose sharply into the sky. Meeting an obstacle in the shape of an unscaleable fence, we climbed towards the road that clings half-way up the hill. Primroses were still in flower and ferns clad a dry burn, but vertigo had me by the throat and my rubber boots had become an intolerable burden to my feet. Reaching the high road, I threw off the boots and changed into plimsoles.

Thirst had become a problem. The quarry yielded no water, but as we descended the Leean   123 a trickle began to play a tune, and led us to a little well, fed by an icy, quenching spring. Cheered by its freshness, we ate a picnic meal, but neglected to fill our flasks from that opportune source.

In front of us, Wasbister lay in sunlight, the pale loch holding a dark island. Heather bells spread a faintly honeyed fragrance, but ling was not yet in flower. Over the wall, halfway down the precipitous field, a ewe had come to grief: four struggling legs kicked in the air. She had rolled into a hollow and become wedged there, being quite unable to extricate herself. Rescued, and set upon her feet, she was at first unable to keep her balance and seemed in danger of rolling headlong into the sea, but as the power came back to her legs she hobbled slowly away, gradually regaining composure.

Behind us, the highest road in Orkney angled up to vanish over the shoulder of Kierfea Hill. In Wasbister we passed rock gardens paved with flags, where a glory of colourful flowers shone and strawberries hid behind nets. A dry milldam blossomed in blue and white with anagallis aquaticus, forget-me-not and water-cress. Farther on, beyond the crossroads, was another picturesque garden, with a thriving bush of juniper flowering over steps of stone.

A windcharger stood on the brae, energetically spinning electricity out of the freshening wind. To the northwest lay the Quandale, with roofless ruins and fallen walls. The gable ends of the first two-storey house in Rousay lifted forlornly. This was a prosperous district in pre-sheep-farming days, for the sea was at hand with abundance of fish; but here, as in the Highlands, sheep were found to be more profitable than people on the land.

On the other side of the road, on the face of the hill, is a district of small grey empty houses where the Quandale people had to settle after their eviction; a bleak and shelterless situation from which to scratch a living, and build new houses from the substance of the Hill.

The roost ran between us and Eynhallow, silver-spangled and white-tipped. At the bend of the road, on the spot where I remembered them, grew field gentians, deeply blue. Here we left the road, crossing the fields towards the Broch of Midhowe and the Stalled Cairn. We were fortunate to find the key to the Cairn, that elusive key which is so hard to track down; a visiting couple had run it to earth, and let us in. We walked around and up the steps, to look down on the brittle stone structure and the burial chambers walled by slabs. A bird had effected an entrance, leaving a very small frail eggshell.

Midhowe is only one of the brochs which have towered along this shore. It stands, well fortified, between two narrow geos, and on the seaward side, as reinforcement, is a piece of modern masonry built with great artistry and precision. Still in search of drinking water I walked along the shore, but although water seeped from one layer of rock for a considerable distance it came only a drop at a time, and green-weeded pools were scarcely inviting. Under a stone, in the remains of another broch, sat a fat, fluffy fulmar which gathered itself to spit.

We came upon a churchyard by the shore, with another stepped-up gate. The ruined church was doorless and also apparently minus windows. It had a strangely sinister air; lichen, long and greeny-grey, hung from its walls. The cemetery was an unchancy place in which to set foot, for there were very few gravestones 125 standing; yet each unmarked grave had a slot at the head where its stone had obviously been uprooted. We saw no sign of the vanished tombstones.

Beside the graveyard, and partly under its wall, we saw the remnant of a castle; steps went down into the mysterious depths of cellar or dungeon, but the opening was too well nettled for investigation.

Leaving this shore of desolation with its ruins of at least four eras, we followed an old road to Westness. The wind had fallen away and stretches of white calm shone on the sea. By the pier at Hullion we renewed acquaintance with a crystal spring of sweet cold water pouring out of the rock face; where we all drank gratefully, despite the presence of some intrusive water-creature which rowed swiftly across its surface. The fulmar-ringers returned, sun-glowing and faintly fish-oil scented. Pleased with our day we crossed the quiet sea, where skarfs and dunters submerged and surfaced. A mellow light of autumn lay on the land.

The Long Hills
of Hoy

One of my periodic extravagances is getting a morning alarm call when I contemplate an early sea trip. There is no other certain means of waking me, because the alarm clock shrills away unheard, or is automatically switched off the moment it begins to dirl. The telephone bell woke me to a mild but midge-infested morning on Friday, and I fed the menfolk and the cats, while issuing instructions as to the table clearing and locking of doors after my departure.

"You'll need this," Donnie said, handing me a tin of insect-repellant spray. I already had a stick of greasy ointment in my bag; I picked up my Thermos, sandwiches and spare shoes, and departed. I soon discovered that I had left without a hanky, which omission to a hayfeverish nose is disaster personified; but my cousin lent me one to be going on with.

Stromness Harbour lay glassily black, with the *St Ola*'s shadow shimmering out towards the gulls who sailed on their reflections. The windows of the new school were darkly translucent like the water, and morning reek rose straight and pale from many chimneys.

Cars were going aboard the *St Ola*, and one sat on the hatch covers of the *Watchful* as we embarked. A merganser dived cleanly, and a tall masted boat swayed on our wash. Ahead of us rose Hoy, hazed and featureless, pasted flatly against the sky.

Suddenly, off Graemsay, two sleek backs broke surface as a pair of porpoises arched and dived. A small flotilla of white feathers floated past, and some green weed. Cormorants passed on dark wings.

Two Devon men were in our company; they were going in search of woundwort, that handsome pink-headed weed that grows near so many houses in Orkney. This is a puzzling species for those who are making a start in botany, because our commonest woundwort is a hybrid between two forms less frequently met in the country. These young men were compiling a thesis on the plant, and were on the outlook for the rarer parents of the hybrid; *stachys sylvatica* which has broad leaves and darker flowers (hedge woundwort); and *stachys palustris* with narrow leaves, no smell and more compact flower spikes (marsh woundwort).

We went close inshore under Bring Head. The weathered sandstone had been shaped by waves and wind, rounded into pillars and carved into gullies. Green scurvy grass contrasted softly with pinkish rock, small bushes clung to the shore's edge, and unidentified yellow flowers made a splash of colour. Bracken grew on a rock-stack, an overflow from the hill above, and one rather intriguing bank of tangles clung together at the base of the cliff. Miles of pale hill land stretched to the west. Rysa and Fara were dark of heather.

If there is any place in Orkney of grimmer aspect than Lyness from the sea, I have not seen it. The scarred hill and the great tanks, derelict piers and desolate concrete remains stand as bleak memorials to the recent past. A ghost-town and a ghost-community, twice-depopulated, lie between the hillslopes and along the shore. But it is far from dead, for sheep, cattle and ponies graze pasture and hill; and, as we watched that afternoon, a busy forage-harvester ate the long green swathes of a sloping field, and packed the shredded goodness for winter-feed. Dwellings were as fresh as paint, but nearby were the reminders of a by-gone age; the roofless grey-stone homes of a crofting race driven, by circumstance, far away.

We were transported southwards, and up a hillroad towards Heldale Water. By the pumping station, near peatbanks where fuel was being loaded on to a tractor, we halted to view the scenery and eat sandwiches. We carried Thermos tea and coffee, which, though hot, were already repulsive and dark-coloured. Soup cubes or Oxo are, perhaps, better subjects for an outing. I had also brought along a sharp fruit drink which was more palatable, but of considerable nuisance value, owing to the extra weight. Half-way back to Lyness I dropped the empty bottle into a convenient hole.

There was a slight breeze which had grounded the midges, but mosquitoes or gnats danced in front of us with their long legs dangling. They were blacker and a size larger than our 'watery midges', but of similar shape. A red-throated diver flew past, and on a little dark-watered lochan another diver swam. We followed the track towards the large loch, through heather scent and gleams of sunlight. The hills rose towards the western sea. By a water tank were signs of occupation; willowherb raised purple spires, and two small apple bushes grew in the heather. There were ferns and woodrush, and tall rashes. Skuas patrolled the loch-shore and hill, but they had lost their springtime aggressiveness and were merely curious about us.

To the southern side of Heldale Water we saw white posts marking an apparent track, but this was not a possible road, as we presumed it to be, but the path of a water-pipe. After following the loch-shore for a short distance we headed up the hill, then down again towards the Burn of Ore.

A large hare sat up on his haunches, staring towards a seated bonxie who faced him, a little way off. Then the hare bounded away with deer-like gait, pursued for some distance by four skuas. The hill-surface was spongy and damp, and broken by almost-hidden water-courses where overhanging banks hid the hollowed-out stream-beds. These were spanned, here and there, by artistically-contrived spider-webs, set to catch small inhabitants of the heath.

Down in the valley we came upon a feast of blaeberries, growing on bushes by a thicket of willow and woodrush. The berries were large and juicy, with a grape-like bloom; they stained our hands and lips purple. Yet, I remember a better berry-patch on the north side of a hill in Rousay, where I could not set a foot down without treading a purple path of fruit. There were crowberries, too, also sweet but full of seeds.

Along the banks of the burn grew willows, bracken, valerian, and ferns; much the same sort of vegetation as that of Syradale, though lacking fuchsia and ivy. Climbing Wee Fea, we came on a long peatbank, shallow at its upper end but deepening towards the bottom, and bedded on the crumbling white stone that gives us sandy roads on many a hill.

On this hilltop, overlooking Lyness, oil tanks have been dug-in, and a wide, rough road winds down the hillside. Here we found New Zealand willowherb, that small, creeping thing, carpeting much of the road surface and sending its seeds flying. One specimen of adder's tongue fern grew there, and wood sage, golden rod and a tallish St John's Wort appeared as we walked downhill.

From our vantage point we viewed the land below, the sheltered plain and the acres of heather and moss. Pale stubble followed the tractor as it gathered silage. Cattle grazed a field where the surface was interrupted by much concrete, and handsome ponies stood nearby. A noisy dog barked as though it had never seen a pair of hill-walkers before in its life.

As the *Watchful* returned, the wind fell away and millions of midges attacked us on the pier. My spray-tin refused to function, and the greasy repellent only trapped a few of them. We breathed midges; they got in our hair, ears, and down our necks. This time, I admit, I was glad to leave the island!

The water lay crystal clear, and, over the ship's side, we saw a vast number of jellyfish-like creatures propelling themselves up and down. They were translucent, with pink tips, and their shape was tubular, unlike genuine jellyfish. At a guess I should say they were some form of sea-squirt.

Before we reached Stromness the weather changed and a cold wind met us. We rose on a swell as we passed Graemsay, and three Norwegian fishing boats were sheltering at the pier.

A Tidal Island

*T*o the ear of the modern reader, the poet David Vedder seems given to hyperbole; yet only the other day a friend remarked, "I don't care whether he's fashionable or no' — I like him!" Now, re-reading his poem "To Orkney," I realise that his exaggeration, if any, is slight. We encounter "whirlpool, torrent, foam" on most sea-journeys. "Oceans meet in maddening shock" where mountainous tides swell in through Westray Firth, and currents plunge over subterranean crags in Burgar Roost and Hoy Sound. "Beetling cliffs" and "shelving holms" are seen throughout the islands, and "dark insidious rocks" menace unwary ships all around our coasts. A "sterile mountain, sered and riven" looms to the west of Stromness, and "yawning gulfs" of gloups and geos may open before our feet on many a cliff-walk.

Nobody need underestimate the power of the tides that race past our shores. The other day, over placid sea, we went to Swona, and in the Firth felt and saw the surges that are never at rest.

The day had a dream quality of clear darkness that was yet brilliant, for patches of deep grey cloud passed over the sea, alternating with bursts of sunshine appearing through fleecy white streamers, so that the water gleamed like darkly rippled silk shot with gold. It was warm to the touch, a fluid, living thing, as it parted to let us through; swelling against the boat in its haste to go somewhere, it tried to divert us from our path. A panorama of sea and islands lay outspread.

Floating like great circular, smooth lilies of grey with dimples in their hearts, the whirlpools were all around us; the Wells of Swona that figure in legend and tale. They did not seek to swallow us, but only pulled strongly against the power of the boat's engine.

To the south-east rose the two Pentland Skerry Lighthouses, one taller than the other. The hill ranges of Orphir and Hoy had receded, but South Walls was clearly visible, and Stroma, full of deserted houses, clung close to Caithness. Beyond Duncansby Head, the Stacks of Duncansby lifted above the land, like a pair of Old Men of Hoy. Ships passed from horizon to horizon.

We drew in to a cosy noust in a sheltered geo. The air had changed; the touch of autumn manifest at home that morning had not reached Swona for a balmy air had come in with that warm tide. We passed through a community of good substantial houses, standing empty on rich black land; habitable houses, where one might seek a haven from the noises of more populous places.There was an atmosphere of perfect peace and contentment on that island, and no sense of desolation, or of isolation, whatsoever. All of our party experienced this; the same benevolent quietude wrapped us round. The traffic of the world was right beside us, too, for up and down the Firth went the ships that travel constantly between the continents, and around the shores of Britain.

We have visited other islands where the sadness of depopulation was evident; it was quite lacking on Swona.

Seals lay ashore in a bay, a colony of dry, furry fellows basking in the sun. Some, on the water's edge, were sleek with sea; they shone in grey, white and pale brown. Others slept in water, their noses tiptilted in air. Eiders stood on stones or paddled in the ebb. The seals surveyed us with great mild eyes, then began to shuffle into the sea, where the whole company turned to watch these interlopers who had appeared on their beach. Whenever I go bird - or beast- watching, I am aware that the subjects of my scrutiny also watch me. Those not unduly wary show a reciprocal interest in the human creature; and perhaps even the flowers through which I tread may be shivering with apprehension lest they are stepped on.

The seals, realising that we were harmless, came sliding slug-like up on shore again, sighing contentedly, grunting, and making odd, childlike cries.

We walked around the headland where the rocks slanted into the sea, and a well edged the shore. A little stone building, roofed and cavelike, was a fish-drying shed, we thought Scilla pods starred the turf, fat with black seeds. While crowberry heather grew in abundance, not a berry remained, though we could see the evidence of avian feasting. Under the banks, the tide ran like a mill-race. A boatload of earlier visitors left the haven.

Turnstone and ringed plover ran over the rocks. Wheatears and rock pipits flew past. Young terns, with greyish plumage, grey and white head markings, and pink feet, stood on a ledge.

We were entertained to tea at the farm, where the garden was scented with Japanese roses, and a glow of red and yellow mimulus lifted to the sun. Lovely yellow kittens played on the brigstones, a large golden tom stood up to be stroked, and a tortoiseshell tapped on the window for admittance, as one of my late lamented cats used to do, long ago.

Walking along the shore towards the chapel and lighhtouse, we passed quoys, or planticrus, where cabbage plants were wont to grow. Here I saw a freak frog orchid, an inch high, with three greenish florets and stunted leaves. Eyebright, very dainty, bushy and small-flowered, grew in the fields and among stones.

The rock strata stood on edge in the ebb, in rows as evenly ridged as ploughed land. On the shore between two seas was the ruined chapel, reputedly as old as Celtic Christianity; here monks have sung and taught, lived in austere humility and tilled their land. Green lichen bearded the stones. There were many buildings on the headland, walls and dykes of comparatively recent date, including fish-drying sheds; but dominating the scene was the small lighthouse. The coastguard hut was nearby. Ships have come to grief along those shores for centuries, ships unaware of reefs and shoals; some through navigational errors; some led astray by fog, or driven by savage seas. On the sea-bed may be galley and galleon; certainly the remains of iron ships can be seen at low tide.

Traces of older occupation became evident as we went further along the craigs. A small, dark-watered loch held an island of reeds; between it and the shore, stones stood on edge. These were not megaliths such as stand in Stenness, and neither were they arranged in circular form. The largest stone pointed to the north, and is aligned to the Pole Star by night; but our amateur archaeologists remained in doubt as to whether those stones were a calendar-observatory (as Stonehenge and the Ring of Brodgar are now believed to be), or the remains of a stalled cairn burial chamber.

The rock scenery was picturesque, the slope of the strata lending itself to geos and pinnacles. Matricaria, whiter than snow, shone in crevices, and birds sailed on air currents. The tide ran ceaselessly offshore, carrying large ships.

We came to a gloup, where rock plants found scant foothold in the slanting walls; the cavern continued under our feet, and, at the cliffward edge, a boat could have entered under the bridge. Shags, sleek and dark, stood, with their paler nestlings, far below.

The sky darkened as we approached the point of departure, and we eased out into a low tide as the shower gathered force. A thunder-plump streamed over us as we forged ahead. The sea was grey and shining; in front were the rose-red and crimson cliffs of South Ronaldsay, while Swona faded to a misty green. The sun broke through the cloud in bars of bright, watery yellow; the passing shower became silvered like herring scales, and a rainbow had its foot on Caithness.

137

Over shore-sea-green, translucent water we entered Sandwick, where bushes edged the banks, and the green mound of a castle rose across the bay. The restless tide-stream flowed through the Firth, around the serene island we had left lying in the sunset beams.

The Deserted Island

The sea had lain still and quiet all week, alternately grey with mist and bright with sun. Saturday dimmed under a heavy drizzle, though a watery gold spread briefly over the evening. A break in the weather was due, we were warned, but Sunday dawned as if made to order, for the north-west wind had cleared the haze and the sky was only streaked in white and grey.

A party of us met at Kirkwall pier, en route for North Faray. Strange as it may seem, I have of late met several people who were unaware of that island's location and even of its existance. Just after the war, while we were living in Rousay, Faray was still tenanted; now it lies lightless, grass-grown and sheep-pastured. Our party that Sunday included a family returning to have a glimpse of their former home which they left seventeen years ago.

We sailed out past ducks and tystes into the tide. Thieves' Holm, situated in the String and receiving its share of sea-gust, is a vivid emerald green, contrasting sharply with the shores of Carness and Stromberry. What peculiar magic is resident in its earth, to keep it so fresh and summer-seeming?

The low west banks of Shapinsay were sheep-clad. Furrows of former cultivation could be seen on the large fields, lying velvet-green like faded plush, turning their backs on the spray; sheep roam a ghostland on these fields, for thirty small crofts were incorporated into the home farm of Balfour Mains. Along this shore is a rock named Grukalty, where according to legend Agricola set foot when voyaging around the ultimate coasts of his Roman Empire, skirting the unconquered territory of the Picts.

We passed between Vasa Skerry and the Ayre, beside the loch where Shapinsay's model yachts sail. The Castle turrets looked over the brae. Still, flat tide-swirls spread all around us, and suddenly we were sailing uphill to meet the tide. A buoy leaned at an angle. Gairsay came steeply up; Grass Holm was as green as Thieves' Holm. Rendall lay squared in gold, green and brown; Hoy rose above Orphir, clad in cloud. Ahead, between Egilsay and Rousay, lifted the clear blue bubble of Fittie Hill. We moved over a sea of shot silk, deep-purple and green.

The Galt Skerry supported a solemn congregation of skarfs, bolt upright and watchful. Approaching the Green Holms, we entered a drier, clearer airstream. A glittering suntrack ran alongside.

Viewed from the sea, Rousay's terraced hillside, which we had climbed a month ago, seemed awe-inspiring. The dark hills of Eday drew near; the tide in Westray Firth pulled against the boat, but the great ocean swells I remembered were not in evidence. Out here on occasion the Firth is filled with tremendous undulations, as if the whole Atlantic were bent on pushing in through this channel to sweep the isles away.

A raincloud gathered over Rousay and the Mainland hills vanished under a shower. Far behind, the Cathedral spire could still be seen. Rusk Holm made a strange spectacle, because the sheep shelter on the skerry appeared directly out of the sea. Sheep on this Holm cross to the skerry at low tide, and the shelter was raised to prevent their being trapped and drowned by the flowing water. Sand shone green below as we nosed in to the boat-slip at Faray and jumped ashore. Several seals, basking on the sand, squirmed and flopped into the sea to eye us from a safer element. The boat moved out to anchor in the bay, and we walked up the grass-grown road.

In the days when Faray folk were content with their island living, the County Council offered them the choice of a road or a pier. Mistakenly they chose the road, and inevitably the island died: now the wide, straight, metalled road runs emptily the length of Faray, with only here and there an outcrop of metalling showing through the recolonising vegetation; past the well-built houses with their broken roofs, the corner-posts that hold fences no more, and the march dykes; dividing the isle, pathway for staring sheep.

We entered a house where the walls stood strongly, now open to the sky. The post that had held a wireless aerial still projected from one chimney; the other, enclosing a small fireplace, 141 opened out surprisingly above: this space had been used for smoking fish. Two knocking stones occupied the yard, and were a fixture there, however much the visitors coveted them! A milldam grew full of waterweeds... here, one winter's night, a horse, loose and running on ice, broke the surface and sank, causing no little consternation...

A sheep had died in the school, and bird-bones lay in the empty water-tank.

We followed the road to Lavey Sound; the rock path connecting Faray and the Holm was still submerged. Rafts of cormorants sat blackly on the sea between us and Eday. The rocks along the east coast slanted steeply into deep water at the same angle as those of Rapness. Clear deep pools were enclosed by great slabs of stone; geos opened suddenly, cutting at sharp angles into the land. The sea murmured and echoed with a subterranean voice, gurgling in caverned stone. A clear, built well on the hillside almost tempted me to drink, but I slaked my thirst on a few crowberries instead: they were the bitterest berries I have ever tasted, bearing no resemblance to the luscious specimens of Rousay.

Examining a tiny plant along the peaty shore, I found myself deserted on an alien beach. A jutting rock enclosed a mass of rotting ware so that the sea was green and thick; beyond, a pool lay crystal clear with every living weed-frond and stone distinct. The shore was divided into layers of conglomerate and red sandstone; petrified pebble-beds held a haphazard shower of little stones as if, falling down an ancient beach, they had been arrested and frozen in mid-avalanche.

I crossed the island to the west shore, shoogling through a bog on the way. Here the rocks stood at a parallel angle to those on the east, slanting inwards and with even more abrupt geos. A fulmar sat on a ledge; sea pinks, campion and lovage throve. Close by the shore was the kirkyard, and we were struck by the nember of young people buried there in the late nineteenth century. Again and again we read of those who died in their teens or as children. What visitation had they suffered: tuberculosis, influenza, or other epidemics? Or were those early deaths the result of an inadequate diet and isolation from proper medical facilities?

No deserted district is a happy place. Thoughts and memories linger around fallen walls and halted wheels. Not a flower remained in a garden; not a tree except dwarf willow grew. From a rocky hillock we surveyed the scene. Sheep followed through the valley, paying us little heed. Down this brae our companions had sledged one Christmas evening, an event remembered by the young man who had been the last bairn born on Faray; and who, in adventurous infancy, once wandered away and was discovered sitting on the edge of a precipitous geo....

We returned to the jetty to see another boat come in to anchor, and a party disembark. The tide was out, the sand lay firm and white, briefly recording our footprints. A colder wind ruffled a wet grey sea as we coasted Eday. In the String we met the hydrofoil, bouncing along at a superior pace like something from the science fiction of my childhood.

"We've had enough sea for one day," said my man firmly as I suggested joining the queue for the next trip. We watched the *Shadowfax* slide effortlessly back to her berth, and under a threatening sky took the west road home.

143

A Field Day at Wharebeth

*T*he last day of September had a bite to it. Showers flew from the nor-west, though the weather had improved somewhat since Friday, when winter-weight torrents had fallen. We left for Wharebeth rather late and found several Field Club cars in the space by the kirkyard. The party had reached the field above the miners' hole and we drove out along the shore road to catch up. There was a better turn-out of members than on most of the summer outings. We climbed a fence, and walked over wet green pasture. Several fences and burns later we took to the shore, where the going had fewer impediments. A burn, with white waterfalls, ran through beds of watercress; its banks were sleeked with water-laid vegetation, and drifts of uprooted cress lay on the rocks below.

A dead gannet was stretched out among   145

the ware. The tide was low, and the firm grey sand shone wetly in the white-gold sunlight. Several years ago the sand of this bay was yellow, but during a stormy winter it migrated to leave a naked, stony beach. The sand that eventually returned had suffered a sea change, and now it lies coldly silver, wave-patterned and worm-whorled, carved by the streams that run down out of the land. Ringed plover and dunlin pattered in the tide's edge. Between us and Breckness, a large seal raised an inquisitive head.

Dandelions were still in flower along the shore with a few buttercups and hawkweeds. White marguerites shone among bright green, fern-like leaves. Most of the cornthistles had seeded, and ranks of dockans edged the beach with iron-red spikes. Goosegrass reached out, intent on distributing its sticky seed-balls by way of passers-by. Small and exquisite, though rather washed-out, autumn-tinted sea-milkwort crept in crevised rock-slabs. The shore had been summer-flushed with sea-pinks; now the dry, papery petals were ghost-pale. The foliage of bird's foot trefoil, and red clover, grew with watercress on a tiny delta of silt where the seeds and soil had run out of the land. Orache was still lush in leaf, and tiny thistle seedlings, in blue-green rosettes, looked, momentarily, like some unknown species that had washed up on a high tide.

Across the tideway rose the Kame of Hoy, and, high above Queen Victoria's silhouette, a burn blew upwards in a small white veil of spray. The water was doing a merry dance, being thrown back on itself only to run down again inthe teeth of the wind. Seen from the sea, this phenomenon has several times been reported by passing ships, as a signal fire on the cliff. Out to sea the horizon rose and fell in hills and valleys of sea, and a river of turbulence ran through Hoy Sound. The mountains of Sutherland came briefly into view, cloud-pale, far west of Hoy.

The shore stones were strewn with bits of wood, smashed fishboxes, fragments of creels, and much drift-plastic. This most indestructible flotsam now clutters every coastline of the world; and unless its components run out, our rocks will in time be hidden by man-made debris. Cast-away bottles eventually become rounded jewels in the sand, and tins rust away; but these plastic objects journey on, gathering barnacles and seaweed, restlessly tide-borne from strand to strand around the globe.

We hunted shells in small sandy coves, between rock-ridges running out from the Breckness shore. Here lay rayed limpets, lined with mother-of-pearl; when I was peedie, we called these 'lady shells'. I found a limpet with a high dome, and many little tortoise-shell limpets ridged in various sea-wet colours. There were top shells, our 'silver Willies', whelks, bright yellow and banded winkles. A dark slab of stone was pock-marked with the holes left by rock-borers. Stone came in many shades and shapes; here lay a smooth-topped square in old-gold, there a slanting, sea-washed area of grey with veins of iron running through it. Leafy, feathery, lacy patterns that might have been designed for fine fabrics, in grey on paler grey, had been laid down in immemorial sediments of ancient seas, to delight us, aeons afterwards, as we chanced to walk thereon. Another held petrified wave-patterns of the past. I stepped upon the slanting surface of brownish rock that held embedded

147

nodules of yellow stone. Wave-rounded granite boulders obtruded through the sand, and pebbles of granite lay for the picking-up.

Just over a fence, in the edge of a field, semi-solid, porous sandstone appeared. I have never been able to decide whether this substance is rock turning into sand, or sand in the process of becoming rock.

Grey and yellow lichens crept on a rock-face where water trickled down from the land. Moss, in cushions of brown and green, occupied the shaded lower strata, and a slime, or algae in brown, rust-red and olive-green, covered the rocks below. Not far away a jellyfish, in colours that almost matched the slime, lay stranded and partially melted, at high water mark. The green, slippery weed that grows where fresh water meets salt, ran down the channelled stone.

Large tangles lay in the ebb. One had been rooted on a stone with a hole in its centre, which fell apart in my hands. Others clung to mussel shells. Bits of bright weed floated in pools by an intrusive dyke.

We walked up to the ruined mansion house of Breckness, that haunted place once belonging to Bishop Graham. Strong walls still faced the elements, and the wide, arched kitchen fireplace looked towards the more recent, now empty farm-house and outbuildings. The mansion had evidently been pillaged of some of its stone when the later buildings were erected, as facings of dressed stone surrounded doors and windows, and ornamented corners.

Buckshorn plantain grew in the old walls, sustained by crumbling plaster. Stone stairs led nowhere now, and iron fastenings had rusted into the stone of the doorway. A great stone lintel lay outside the front hall, where the windows have a panoramic view of Hoy, the Sound, and the western sea.

On the upper face of the cliff below we saw masonry, the inner wall of a broch; a fallen, former fortress which would have had an equally commanding view of the seaward approaches. Further along, square, stone-lined drain openings jutted out of the black earth. Here was manifest evidence of the sea's encroachment over the past 2,000 years. The crags were undercut, and I came upon a small cave that had been scooped and smoothed out by ages of wave and tide-swirl. Here, above the ware, a restless company of shore-flies flitted to and fro. No doubt there was method in their meanderings, though they seemed to lack purpose or direction.

Lime grass was fresh and green on the banks, and in the fresh wind and sunlight an illusion of spring still lingered on. Back in the car, we watched the sea. Sunlight lay gold on the heaving horizon, and Scotland had vanished; then, as the clouds shifted, a shadow mountain massif appeared. At the foot of the Kame, waves reared up intermittently over some unseen rock. The scene was fluid with changing light; now the whole bay was filled with blinding brilliance, then a grey cloud shaded the sea to let the green sand gleam through under thin sunbeams. The sand shone, coldly silver, and the small waders still ran darkly between the redware and the watered sand.

Pilgrims on the
Brough of Deerness

*A*fter a bad forecast came a grey Sunday, the first of October. White waves were on the loch and clouds passed swiftly. Tones of gold and crimson lay over the swamp, and the trees were changing; there were drifts of leaves in Finstown although gardens were still bright. A black duck swam in the bay.

We passed fields heavy with stooks on green new grass, and one stack stood on gold stubble, conspicuous among so many waiting sheaves. Gold-tinselled corn-thistles grew by the road; green tufts of rashes covered a pale field. Toadstools by the thousand had erupted from a silage pit; this is a toadstool year, for the mild damp weather has brought into being a multitude of varied fungi, many of them lovely in their peculiarly loathsome frailty. Frilled specimens, looking as though formed of coiled gossamer, with a tenuous grasp of the earth, have sprung up in our wet grass. Orange ones, more substantial and uneven in shape, now lie browning at the edges. Little saucer-shapes, pink tinged, and high-domed white things that shivered as we trod near them, appeared frequently during our Sunday walk. But when silage sprouts fungoid growths, what happens to the kye who eat it?

Two small boats sailed in the String, on a white-shot grey sea that was green and purple inshore where sand and seaweed lay. Flocks of birds were on the wind, in disc shapes that expanded and contracted their way into the distance. I wonder if some of these incredible-sounding U.F.O.'s that, according to a few dedicated sky-watchers, change shape and direction with amazing alacrity, may not be flights of migrants high in the sky?

Kirkwall's gardens wore gay flowers. A pair of ponies watched us over a wall. Rooks rode air-currents above brown-edged trees.

A field near Grimsetter was deeply tractor-marked between its rows of stooks. Hangars were silver in the sun now breaking the cloud. Lichened trees, like beldames old and droll, raised withered arms by the balley of dragons' teeth. Kye grazed among rashes. A blaze of orange montbretia shone by a garden thickly elder-hedged.

In Toab harvesting was in progress; stacks were rapidly rising. Tractors drew heavy square loads; sheaves flew from forks, and folk smiled thankfully. Tatties stood in sacks on black land.

Dragons' teeth studded the sand. Lime-grass waved tough-stemmed seed-heads, its pale green foliage beginning to change to a sandy gold. In Deerness, fields were closely stooked. A flock of plover rose, shining, and a wheatear flashes from a fence. We made a detour down a new road, then returned to the main highway, to see the Field Club members already congregated at Skaill.

There were flowers in the sand for the bairns to list and collect; bugloss and sea-rocket, charlock, dead nettle, annual nettle; and a glowing red patch of orache as bright as any autumnal tree. Sea-purslane and silver-weed foliage were turning to gold. A burn-bed yielded a rare plant, water-whorl, grass, and a delicate-looking, slender-branched sea-pearlwort, close relative of a troublesome tiny weed, yet a thing of beauty in its own place. Burns cut sharp-edged tracks through the sand, and the largest of these, flowing past the house on the shore, was vividly green with water-starwort and water-cress.

Here we found a garden overgrown by comfrey, nettles and dockans. The house was untenanted but sound. A huge iron buoy surmounted a concrete base. The leaves of mimulus appeared in the burn. Vivid red campion still bloomed on the cliff's edge, and a number of black sheep grazed nearby. Out to sea, behind us, rose Copinsay and the Horse; dark craigs challenged them on the Deerness shore. The kirkyard perched on the shore's edge at Skaill, with the kirk's yellow-lichened roof repeating the autumn tones of the land.

A waterfall ran into the Gloup at one end, and the sea came swelling in at the other end, under our feet. Down the sides of this awesome hole grew sheltered greenery - grasses hanging sleekly, woodrush, scurvy-grass, and a very handsome angelica in seed, its leaves wine-red and oat-gold. Ragwort, bush vetch and spear

153

thistle grew around its edge, the thistles bursting full of soft-plumed seeds. Creeping willow, those miniature hanging trees, fringed the burn, and crowberry spread in the heather, its berries few.

Silver-weed was now silvery-grey, its leaves curling against the wind. On the wet moor between the Gloup and the Brough were found adders' tongue fern and frog orchid. We halted on the shore while the first few members scaled the path leading to the Brough.

This is a most venerable place which I cannot in all honesty describe, because I did not attempt to climb the narrow path. Of old, pilgrims crept up it on their hands and knees; a practice which may have been due as much to caution as to sanctity. The first occasion on which I visited the Brough was in 1956, at this time of year and in much the same climatic conditions. Then, I wanted to climb on to the peninsula but my man dissuaded me. This time he made the ascent while I remained in the geo, contemplaing cliffs and the sea.

The remains of a landward-facing wall could be seen, running around the top of the Brough. From the opposite cliff-top we observed signs of buildings, which are sinking into the untouched turf; no beast can get across to eat the grass, and generations of vegetation have flourished and died to form a deep spongy undergrowth from which rise the foundations of monastic cells, chapel, and other buildings pertaining to the various shades of religion of who-knows-how-many centuries.

Now, did the peace that seeped into my being come only from the calmness of the afternoon and the swell of the waves, or did the very rocks give forth a blessing? Centuries of prayer and meditation have hallowed this place; but was it chosen because of its atmosphere, or is this atmosphere something that was given to it? Here the early Christian monks have meditated upon the very boulder on which I sat; and certainly they have fished from that rock where brown and gold weed moved, and limpets clung; where whelks crawled, and barnacles had prisoned themselves in crusted colonies to give grip to feet walking over a slippery surface.

The sea lapped a tongue of rock and sounded into a cave. A semi-detached rocky headland, giving shelter from the south-east, grew fine green grass, sea-pinks, and yellow lichen. Geological faults slanted down the face of the Brough, the intrusive rocks red-iron stained. At my hand were strange, grey-black honeycomb strata, down which had dripped, aeons ago, strings of honey-coloured quartz.

A seal swam in swelling black water, and turned its sleek head to look at me. Ripple-marks of an ancient sea corrugated a stone. I picked up two pebbles, scarlet and white-streaked, that had come out of the dyke at my feet. The pilgrims descended the narrow path, and the spell was broken.

Twenty-Fower
Herrin Barrels

*M*y great-great-grandfather was one John Skea of Sanday. Close on two hundred years ago he left that low-lying island for a change of scene. Setting sail in a fishing smack, he made landfall on Shapinsay, where he thought the grass grew greener. He was a crofter-fisherman and a handloom weaver, and his age was nineteen.

The house of Osted lay in a sunward valley, where the gold of kingcups ran down the burn to the sea. Five nousts, then harbouring the herring fleet, nestled in the lee of a low headland. On a stony brae was the Kettle Quarry, where the fishers barked their nets by steeping them in cauldrons of brown preservative. There was a well of clear water and a good pond by the shore, and the southeast wind, aided by the tide, carried much sea-wrack into the bay. But

157

the house and out buildings had fallen into disrepair, and much of the land had never felt a plough.

Although the situation appealed to him in its resemblance to his Sanday home at Pool, John had second thoughts about living where the thatch above his head might vanish in a winter gale, while he slept with the seawind crying under the sagging flagstones of his neuk-bed. The cow bogled in her draughty stall. John, after giving the croft a fair trial, flit his few belongings to Purtaquoy, on the edge of the wet moor, which proved even less to his liking in spite of the ample peat-supply by his door.

By this time he had found himself a wife, Cecilia Drever. Restlessly, he again moved on, having obtained a few acres on the far side of the island, in the West Hill Field, where he raised for his bride and his handloom a home of his own making. Here, at Shuttlefield, their family grew.

John was a small and agile man, who could turn his hand to any trade. In his early teens he had gone to sea with the herring boats, for this was the heyday of the herring, prior to the coming of the trawlers that swept away the inshore fishing. It was a hard and perilous life driving out to sea with wind-filled sails, hauling nets rich with a cold and gleaming harvest, while hands, cracked with salt, spilt blood among the fish.

To Stronsay's curing station there came in season a thriving fleet of fishers, and flocks of rough-handed and rougher-tongued lasses who cleaned, salted and packed the fish.

The fisher lads, for relaxation, invented their own games, one of which was barrel-jumping; this was popular all around the coast, while barrels were waiting to be filled.

Two dozen empty herring barrels stood in a row on Stronsay pier. In the quiet of the evening several youths had gathered to tease the girls and to show off. Old men leaned on the wall, smoking clay cutties and telling great lies about their feats of strength, and their courting escapades, in past days.

"Na, min, times are changed", said one, wagging his grey beard. "I mind the day - "

"Luk at Jock Skea jumpan!" cried another, "Man, that's a soople fellow! I h'ard o' a West Heilan' man that jumped in an' oot a dizzen barrels; Jock, here's a hale shillin for thee if thoo can bate that!"

The result was to become a legend among the fishermen. John leapt lightly into the first barrel; close-footed, he bounded out and into the second. In and out, in and out he sprang, down the twenty-four herring barrels lined up on Stronsay pier.

John's first youth was past before he left the fishing and built his home. Shuttlefield was not a long-time anchorage; by the decree of a progressive landlord its small fields were swallowed up by the larger farm of Balfour Mains: the home farm of the Balfours, which incorporated thirty homes of crofters. But before this took place John had returned to Osted which was again vacant; there he planned to make a permanent dwelling by tearing down the decrepit buildings and erecting a better house on the face of the brae known as Brek Tooan. The weaver-seaman built his home and steading with long, low walls facing the sea. He quarried stone that was still the property of the estate although he broke it from the flat rock slabs of the shore, and of the original house only the steethe remained, sunk into the green.

John and his sons hauled seaweed ashore to manure their fields, and burnt tangles to make kelp which helped to pay the rent. The spring-time hill yielded peats for their year-long fires. They drank the rich brown ale, home-brewed from their own malt, which they dried in their round kiln; and this was the essence of their harvest, relished with the oatcakes, bere-bannocks, salted meats and dried fish that formed their staple diet. They fished sillocks and cuithes from the rocks and rowed their boat to sea, and the days wove themselves into a pattern as the threads flew behind the shuttle. The cruisie lamp lit their evenings and the firm walls kept out the salted gales.

John's elder son, John, married and found himself another home. David, my great-grandfather, grew up to be a seaman, and a mason, dyking for the Laird; he became a noted killer of pigs, those rough-fed hogs that rooted through every township to the disgust of certain parish historians, but filled the winter pickle-barrel for the benefit of the population.

Despite their sunward-facing valley and the generous tide, life's troubles did not always pass them by. Smallpox came to the house, and although nobody died, young Cecy was left so badly pock-marked that no man ever sought her hand. A remedy not far removed from witchcraft was used on the sufferers when 'the old folk' gave them roasted mice to eat.

Then came John's adventure in the Sooth Country, an experience such as may happen in a family but once in living memory; and while memory lives a long time tales lose nothing in the telling.

They sat at their evening meal of brose, bannocks and freshly boiled partans caught in the ebb, when the letter arrived. John could neither read nor write, but David was sufficiently schooled to read his Bible, the Coats' library books, and to keep his accounts. Cecy was also a voracious reader, who read her way through all the library books, and discoursed upon them afterwards; this in an age when book-learning was held to be of small account. They stared open-mouthed at the letter.

"Fether," asked David, "Didno' thoo hiv' an uncle John that gaed tae sea?"

"Aye, boy I did! Bit wir no heard o' him for many a year."

"Weel, he's deed, an' he's left thee some property. I'm gaun tae shaw this paper tae the minister, for I canna believe me eyes!"

But David had made no mistake. The uncle, whose travels in foreign parts had proved highly profitable, had died in London leaving his nephew a fortune: a row of houses, several shops, and a considerable sum of money.

"Weel, David, I'll go tae the toon an' tak ship for London," the heir decided.

"An' thoo'll pen them a letter, sayan I'm on me way."

John still had his seaman's certificate. He worked his passage by stages, having to make a detour to Antwerp on the way, because no direct transport then existed between the Northern Isles and the cities of the South. The journey took six weeks, while David and his mother and sister delved, spun, and tended the beasts as they were wont to do. David rose in the small hours to comb the shore for driftwood, and his mother baked her bread by cruisie-light long before the dawn. The boy set out to visit his lass late of an evening, when older folk were abed;

161

and by devious routes he travelled, lest any crony see him go!

The tall ship came up the Sound, running before the tide and wind. John stepped ashore on Kirkwall pier, and found an island fishing smack to take him home; and as they tacked and veered to make landfall he reflected on his fortune, the golden guineas in his pocket, the papers safe inside his seaman's jacket.

"Whit's this?" demanded his son. "Are thoo lost thee senses, Fether? Someone's dune thee oot o' a' thee property! Thoo should hae sent me; at least I could hiv' read this paper!"

"Dune me oot o' it? Whit wey? I met twa gentlemen on the docks, dressed as weel as the Laird, an' they tuk me tae a grand hoose an gaed me a dram or twa. Then wan fellow tuk this paper oot o' the drawer an' wrote me name on it; he said the ither man was a witness; an' all I hed tae dae was mak me cross? See, there it is, John Skea, his mark! Then they said it wis all settled noo, gaed me a haep o' gold money tae tak' home an' anither dram. Why wid fine upstandan men like that swindle me, efter bein' so kind?"

"I doot yin London gentry gaed thee a dram right enough," said his son grimly, and snatching up the documents with their heavy impressive-looking seals, he strode across the Glebe lands towards the manse.

"I see little hope of redress," said the minister, "for I cannot advise another London trip for your father, even if he could find these men again. Such a pair of rogues would not hesitate to use violence, and he is obviously unused to the ways of the world. You had better forget the whole affair. There are wolves in many a seaport tavern, David, waiting for lambs to fleece!"

But while they toiled they did not forget, and the papers lay in a box for two generations as proof of John's voyage and its outcome; then, after the family had been visited by a fever, Cecy burnt them in her ritual cleansing of the house.

"What you never have you never miss," they say, and that was the carefree attitude of John Skea who philosophically took life as it came, and whose days were long on the land. He died, tranquil and full of years, at the age of ninety-seven, after a sunny summer spent drowsing daily in a chair in the lee of the garden dyke. But while a lost fortune may soon be forgotten by a community, someone always remembers the athletes of the past. Long years after John and David had gone to their rest in the grey-walled kirkyard, old men would laugh at lads leaping over dykes, and think of a story recounted long ago: "Did thoo ever hear tell o' Jock Skea, that jumpid in an' oot o' twenty-fower herrin barrels on the Stronsay pier?"

Grandad's Boat

He was a crofter and a fisherman:
   He built his boat with canny craftsman's skill;
Delving and building up his patch of land,
   Slicing cold fuel from the dark, springtime hill.

With mason's hands he raised grey stone on stone:
   Walls with grey mortar firming to the gale.
Green moved his pasture to the wind's moan,
   Proudly his shining boat spread her new sail.

Out through the tideway into the sunrise;
   Bright moves the water, leaping behind;
Shining with fish scales, heavy the boat lies
   Smoothly the oars ply home through the wind.

Low in the valley the house waits his coming:
   Over the dark rocks the red tangles move:
Into the boat-noust the young craft is homing:
   Bright race his bairns on their swift feet of love.

Many the skate, and the cuithe, and the codling:
   Many the voyage on pathways of sea:
Grey is the old man, and heavier his rowing;
   Down drag the years, and the toiler is free.

Snug in her haven the old boat is waiting,
   Sailing in dreams on that bright lifting tide,
Bearing a spirit on wings of the morning,
   Fain to be seaworthy, outward to glide.

Time-rotted timbers through two generations,
   Falling and mouldering in sight of the seas:
Youthful and reverent, the fourth generation
   Carry his boat home to rest by his trees.